I AM
GOING TO
BE DEBT
FREE

First published in 2013 by
Liberties Press
7 Rathfarnham Road | Terenure | Dublin 6W
Tel: +353 (1) 405 5701
www.libertiespress.com | info@libertiespress.com

Trade enquiries to Gill & Macmillan Distribution
Hume Avenue | Park West | Dublin 12
T: +353 (1) 500 9534 | F: +353 (1) 500 9595 | E: sales@gillmacmillan.ie

Distributed in the UK by
Turnaround Publisher Services
Unit 3 | Olympia Trading Estate | Coburg Road | London N22 6TZ
T: +44 (0) 20 8829 3000 | E: orders@turnaround-uk.com

Distributed in the United States by
Dufour Editions | PO Box 7 | Chester Springs | Pennsylvania 19425

ISBN: 978-1-907593-44-4
2 4 6 8 10 9 7 5 3 1

A CIP record for this title is available from the British Library.

Cover design by Ros Murphy

Internal design by www.sinedesign.net

Printed by Bell & Bain Ltd., Glasgow

I AM GOING TO BE DEBT FREE

DON'T JUST CHANGE YOUR
FINANCIAL LIFE – TRANSFORM IT

LIAM CROKE

Contents

For my parents, Paul and Madeline

Introduction

Do you find it hard to sleep at night, worried that you won't be able to repay your mortgage this month or that you don't have enough money to heat your home – again? It is an awful feeling – and so frustrating that no matter what you do to cut back on your spending, or how hard you work, you never seem to have enough money to live on each month; there is too much month at the end of the money.

So what are you going to do about this situation? What do you have to do to get on top of your finances? What steps do you have to take to figure a way out of the mess you are in?

Well, first things first: you are not alone. This is probably of little comfort to you, but I meet people every day who tell me before we get to speak about their finances that 'you have never met anyone as bad as me before'. You know what? I have. I have met so many people who think that their situation is so bad, so unmanageable, that they don't see any point in even talking about their finances. What I find sad about cases like this is that the people involved seem to have given up on *themselves* rather than on their finances.

These people are amazed when I tell them that I have seen worse, or when I ask them: 'Is that all the debt you have?' Some people have a mental block, believing that their debt is worse than anybody else's, and they are resigned to being permanently in debt, with no escape, ever!

Let me give you a quick example of this. (By the way, I am going to be giving you real-life examples throughout this book that you will be able to relate to, and be inspired by.) Recently, I met a man called John, who came to me looking for help because he was about to lose his job. John was probably one of the smartest guys I have ever met, but before he even sat down to speak with me, he said: 'I don't know why I am even here. Nobody can help me; I'm just wasting your time.'

'That's fine,' I replied. 'If you want to leave without telling me your story, that's up to you, and then you are absolutely right – neither I nor anybody else will ever be able to help you, that's for sure.'

He was taken aback by my reply. I'm sure he thought he was going to get the sympathy hearing from me, but if he thought this he was sadly mistaken. 'Tell me what's wrong, John,' I continued, 'and let's see if I can help you. It's up to you.'

John explained that he was losing his job not because he couldn't do it properly – he could do it with his eyes closed – and not because his employer was laying off people, but because his work was suffering very badly because he could only give it 20 percent of his concentration, time and effort. The other 80 percent was spent worrying about his finances. He was paralysed by his debt and what the future held for him. He had two young children, he hadn't put oil in the tank for twelve months, and his relationship with his wife was at breaking point. He was in a very dark place and saw only one escape route that would put everyone at peace. You know what he was thinking of doing, so let's not even go there for the moment.

John thought that his debt was insurmountable. I'm sure you are thinking it must have been enormous. Well, to John it was: it was €12,000. Yes, you read it right: twelve thousand euro.

To cut a long story short, after many sessions with John, and after putting a plan in place for him that would eliminate this debt once and for all, he did it in January of this year. John and his family are now debt-free apart from a small mortgage, which is very manageable. He is employed again and is one of his new employer's most valuable employees. He is enjoying life again and is a completely different person. His relationship with his wife has changed for the better, and in August of this year John and his family are going on a family holiday together for the first time in years, all paid for in cash from their savings.

Two years ago, he was 'broke': he had no prospect of a job and was €12,000 in debt, and his mortgage was two months in arrears. Now he is debt-free and has €5,000 in savings in his bank account.

How John solved his problems was not down to me, it was down to him. You, and only you, can get yourself out of debt and live the life you want. The great thing is that I have met many thousands of Johns over the past twenty years, and what I show them, and what I am going to tell you now in this book, works, it's a proven fact.

If you follow what I am going to show you, I guarantee that your financial well-being will improve dramatically: it simply can't but improve. However, you have to look yourself in the mirror and say: 'OK, I hear what Liam has said and I am going to follow his plan, and if I do, I am going to be debt-free.' Say it again: 'I am going to be debt-free.'

As you read each chapter in this book, you are going to learn very quickly where your problems lie, and how you got to this point in the first place. But the most important thing is that I am going to show you a way out of debt, and how never to return there again. As Lynsey Buckingham says: 'Been down one time, been down two times, never going back again.'

Let me tell you one more thing which is very important to know about me, the person giving you this advice. I am debt-free apart from a very small mortgage which I could clear at any time. I am not beholden to anyone, and I made a conscious decision to become this way a number of years ago. I have never been in debt and have never been in arrears. You are not getting advice from someone who has made loads of money and then lost all of it again. You are not getting advice from someone who is telling people how to get rid of their debt but is up to their own eyes in debt.

I always find it strange why people would take advice from someone who is in debt themselves or someone who made millions in the 'Celtic Tiger' era, only to have lost it all. Why would you take advice from someone who has failed at managing their own money? If you were on a diet, would you take advice from someone whose weight was going up and down along with yours? Of course you wouldn't. The same applies to your finances: you mimic and copy the people who lived prudently and have successfully managed their own finances, and have *never* made mistakes. These are the people you need to take advice from, and I am happy to say that I am one of them.

Over the course of this book, I am going to show you how to avoid the debt traps that people fall into, and how to create a realistic spending plan that works for *you*. I guarantee that you will find the answers you have been looking for. You will see that my proven plan for a debt-free life will alter your life dramatically for the better and allow you to pursue what you really want from your life, finding out what your passion really is and pursuing it, free from debt and the consequences that debt brings.

I am reminded of a quote I heard recently which goes something like this: 'The mass of men lead lives of quiet desperation.' So make a commitment now not to remain one of those people who struggle throughout their lives, living unfulfilled and never reaching even 10 percent of their potential because they were strangled by debt that dragged them down year in, year out. You are not going to let that happen to you. I want you to say this sentence out loud once more: 'I am going to be debt-free.'

I like quotes, and will use many of them throughout this book to amuse and inspire you. One that I came across recently (the author was unknown) I think is very apt in relation to what I have just been talking about: 'Life is not about waiting for the storm to pass . . . it's about learning how to dance in the rain.'

So, your storm (debt) is going to pass, but rather than waiting for that to happen, let's do something about it now, and let's get on top of your finances so you can get on with the rest of your life. By reading this book, you are taking the first steps to achieving this.

Some people believe that only wicked or lazy people experience money problems. Rubbish. Bad things happen to good people. So, first things first: if you think that you, or someone you know, deserves the problems they are having, now is the time to let go of that negative, judgemental idea. You or your friend has just tripped over some of life's hurdles instead of gliding over them, that's all.

For years I have been helping people find solutions to difficult money problems, and in every single case there was a solution to overcome their problem, no matter how difficult it appeared to be. The same applies to you.

Unfortunately, many people make the mistake of insisting on tackling their money problems alone. Without the right knowledge, experience and tools, this can be like trying to defuse a landmine. If you have never done that before, it can lead to an unintended outcome that isn't pretty.

There really isn't much good information out there about the reality of financial problems. I have watched people struggle alone with financial problems many times, and it's not pretty. It's like standing at the side of the railway track waiting for a train wreck to happen, and knowing that it could have been avoided.

The advice in this book is about helping you avoid going off the rails and guiding you towards your solution. If you are shown the right path, and follow it, you will start enjoying life again.

There are many other books on personal finance, and every single one of them only provides you with information. That's it. The people who write these books are doing you no service at all: they are not going to change your life, I assure you. Information alone will not solve your financial problems.

My formula for financial success is simple:

Knowledge + Action = Power

So, this book is transformational, not informational. My advice is full of honest, hard-learned facts that everyone needs to know when tackling financial difficulties. It really is the stuff that you wish someone had told you before you learned the lessons the hard way. So no matter how hard things may be now and over the course of the next few months, I promise you that if you do what I tell you to do, you will be enjoying life again much sooner than you ever imagined.

This book is a bit like joining a health club to improve your body. It's not enough just to buy membership and never use it. You have to work out; you have to exercise.

OK, let's get started.

'I was part of that strange race of people aptly described as spending their lives doing things they detest, to make money they don't want, to buy things they don't need, to impress people they dislike.'

–Emile Henry Gauvreau

01

Why People Get into Debt

Most people think getting into debt is easy: you simply spend more than you earn. It seems pretty obvious, doesn't it? If you want to stay in the black, then just pay your bills and don't overspend. Most people think getting into serious debt is something that only happens to careless people, people who spend far more than they should and ignore the bills. That, of course, is not necessarily the case.

There are two main ways that people find themselves overwhelmed by their debt:

Unavoidable debt

Some people get into debt quickly and suddenly, through losing their job, losing their business, confronting a medical issue where they can't work, or experiencing some mental or emotional trauma. This can result in a double whammy: they are unable to work (or earn) for a time.

Avoidable debt

There are ten times as many people in this category as in the first one. For these people, the debt just sort of 'sneaked up' on them, over years of unhealthy financial behaviour. There are three types of people in this group.

Firstly, there are those who choose not to think about it – they simply choose to spend without thinking, buying things they don't need with money they don't have. Excessive spending is probably the single biggest reason I have encountered for people getting into debt in the first place.

For some, it is like an addiction to alcohol or drugs. Like these vices, it can, and does, interfere with every aspect of your life, including damaging what could be most precious to you: the relationships with the people you love the most. Or some people make a wrong financial decision, such as a bad investment, having done little or no research. (I see this happen all the time.)

Secondly, many people get into debt through self-denial or blind hope. These people know what they are doing but think (or hope) that things will get better, and spend as if things already *are* better, or at least before they have got better . . . if they ever do.

Finally, many people get into debt simply because of their ignorance: they don't know how much their credit is costing them, or the implications of 'minimum payments'. Their lack of financial education catches them out.

Whether you are in debt because of unavoidable situations or avoidable choices, debt is debt, and it is much harder getting out of it than getting into it – just like weight loss.

Trust me on this: some people get into debt subconsciously, and for what feel like good reasons at the time. Lack of self-esteem, enabling, addiction, keeping up with the Joneses, or whatever else: the reasons behind what drove you to where you are today are significantly more important than the amount of debt people have got right now. Why? Because if you don't figure out how and why you got where you are right now – and resolve these issues – you will find yourself sabotaging your progress and winding up right back where you started.

This might sound odd, but my heart goes out to those people of above average income who suddenly 'hit the wall', because the more you have, the farther you have to fall, and you also have the emotional baggage to deal with. Just because someone lived a good life, or lived comfortably, doesn't mean they don't need help when things go wrong. But for this type of person, looking for help or admitting to a problem is very difficult.

Why am I talking about how you got into debt? Identifying why you got into debt in the first place will help, in the long term, to release you from debt. It is not enough to get out of debt; you also have to *stay* out of debt so that you can build the life you and your family deserve. Trust me when I tell you this: it will require a big shift in the way you previously thought and managed your money in the past. You have to start thinking and acting differently. If you are on a diet, what good is it to lose weight if you put it all back on again?

Debt is like fat in your finances: it weighs you down, it stops you from achieving your financial goals, and it can even end up costing you your life. Don't let this happen to you: it's time to shed the fat now.

Before you can shed any of your debt problems, you first need to understand how you got into trouble in the first place. If we don't take the time to find out how you got into this state, then the likelihood is that you will make the same mistakes again and again.

Think back to a time when you were able to live on a salary without ever having to borrow extra money or go into overdraft. What happened that made you get into debt in the first place? Did you lose your job? Did you buy a house, or houses, that you really couldn't afford? When the bank pre-approved you for loans, or the credit card company increased your limit, did you go on a spending spree? Maybe your debt was caused by a combination of a number of factors.

When I meet people and ask them how they are, the majority of people always answer in the same way: they will tell you that they are great, doing really well, and very busy. Whether this is in fact true or not, we all want the world to think that we are doing well; we never want to admit that things are not great or that we are having a bad day.

I come across people all the time who are driven by the need to prove to the world how well they are doing through the things they have: a big house, a new car, a property abroad, a 50-inch plasma television, and so on. (By the way, a large percentage of these people want to make the choice of trading down their car or house in order to save for better things in the future.) However, they want to keep the trappings of wealth, and feel ashamed, or a failure, if they cannot keep up, on the financial front, with their friends.

Let me tell you this: it takes courage to choose to have second-best right now in order to have the best in a few years' time. But most of us are not courageous; we are controlled by what others think about us.

About five years ago, before I decided to live a life free of debt, I drove a brand-new, top-of-the-range Mercedes. It cost about €55,000 and the monthly repayments were about €1,000 per month. I think I drove this car – no, in fact I *know* I drove (and bought) this car – for reasons of vanity. Here I was, 'cock a hoop', driving my swanky black Merc.

My awakening came one day when I was looking at what the cost was going to be of putting my three girls through college in the years ahead. Jesus, €40,000 each! How in the name of God will I be able to save this when I don't really have any money left over at the end of each month? As I pondered this, I looked out of my living room window and saw my Merc sitting in the drive – where it had been sitting for twenty-three hours out of twenty-four each day – it dawned on me instantly how stupid I was to be putting vanity over my children's education. The following day, I brought the car to a local garage and, luckily, sold it for the amount I owed on it at the time.

I now drive a six-year-old car, but I don't owe anything on this car. And you know what? It gets me to my office just as quickly as the Merc did. Now when I look out at this car in my drive, it gives me a great feeling to know that I owe nothing on it and that I have no monthly repayment to make to a finance company. In fact, I get more pleasure from it than I used to get from the Merc.

But I didn't stop paying that €1,000 per month; I kept doing it. But rather than making a bank rich, I was putting the money into a savings account and making sure that I could financially help my children – by paying for their college education – in the years ahead.

I now have enough money to pay for two of my three kids' education, and I will have enough money for the third in three years, nine months. There was really no choice. A car or my kids' education: it's no contest.

I also don't care about what other people might think of my six-year-old car. In fact I know they don't think anything of it, because I look after it, clean it, and get it serviced regularly. Except for the fact that it has an '06' registration number, you would think it was a new car.

When I tell this story at seminars, I like to give the audience a visual description of what the Merc was costing me. My loan repayments were supposed to be €1,000 per month, and I had it financed over five years, i.e. sixty months. There are 1,825 days in five years. If you divide the number of days by the cost of the car, you get 32.88. My car was costing me €32.88 per day, so every day for the next five years I might as well roll down the window and throw €32.88 out into the road, because that is exactly what I was doing.

How much are you throwing out the window each day? Can you afford to keep doing that? I want you to keep the picture in your mind of me rolling down my car window and throwing €32.88 into the abyss every single day. I also want you to keep a picture of me in your mind driving to my bank and depositing €32.88 into a savings account every day. Which person do you want to be? Which person are you going to be?

Before I continue, say out loud for me again: 'I am going to be debt-free.'

How do I know if I have a serious debt problem or if I am headed that way?

There are many people whose level of debt has got to the stage where no matter how much they cut back and watch what they spend their money on, or no matter how closely they monitor their account, they still find themselves increasing their debt for a variety of reasons, or, worse still, they start missing monthly loan commitments.

I am going to outline some warning signs below. If these are happening to you frequently, I am very glad you are reading this book.

- You are juggling or even ignoring bills until you start getting final reminders.
- You are receiving phone calls at home or letters from finance companies about arrears on your account.

- You are using your credit card more frequently to buy food and petrol.

- You are hiding the true level of your accumulated debt from your spouse.

- You are constantly living in your overdraft.

- Christmases and birthdays are not as happy as you would like them to be because you worry about how you are going to pay for gifts or how you are going to pay back the money you borrowed to buy them in the first place.

- You are thinking about your financial predicament 24/7.

- You are looking for new credit but have been refused because of a poor credit history.

There is no specific level of debt that should trigger you seeking help and doing something about your finances. It does not matter if your debt is €1,000 or €50,000, what matters is how committed you are to getting out of the situation you find yourself in. When it comes to money, winning is 80 percent about behavior and 20 percent about head knowledge. Most of us know what we should be doing but we just don't do it.

So, why do people fail to get out of debt even if they are completely committed to doing so? The reason is very simple: they refuse to set up and actively maintain a budget. This is an area that I am going to cover comprehensibly in the book. But before I do, I think we need to look at the different stages of debt that everyone goes through.

'We can pay our debts to the past by putting the future in debt to ourselves.'

—**John Buchan**

02

The Five Stages of Debt

It is widely recognised that when you get into debt, you pass through various stages. How people go through each stage is very much up to them. However, no matter what stage you are at, or how you are dealing with it, the most important thing you have to do is to take action to resolve the difficulty you are in. I can certainly help you with this, but you have to take action yourself and you have to be determined to take back control of your life. So what I need from you now is determination, resolve and belief that you are going to overcome your debt problems.

Let's look at the various stages people go through when they are faced with debts they cannot afford to repay, and how they react.

1. Denial

This is the first stage that people go through. Believe me, you don't have to be in debt to be in this stage. I see it happen all the time, and hear comments such as 'It won't happen to me' or 'I will never get myself into that situation' all the time.

Deep down people know that they are on a slippery slope and that their situation is getting out of control, but they bury their heads in the sand and hope that the situation they find themselves in will miraculously improve. They are fooling no one but themselves, and they start to confuse facts with opinions (and think things like 'My house will never be repossessed', 'My lender will offer me debt forgiveness' and 'I can't afford to take my child out of private school').

I always tell people that they must understand the difference between facts and opinions, because if they don't, they end up doing insane things and begin to take risks that may take them years to recover from – or, worse still, which they may never recover from. I firmly believe that denial is the reason for this.

Listen to me when I tell you some facts: denial of your debts will make your situation much worse. If you think you have money problems, listen to your gut instinct, because it's right: you have problems. And if you think you have time on your side, you are sadly mistaken. You don't: time is your enemy. You have to take action as fast as possible, because the more time you spend in denial, the worse your problem is going to become. You simply have to get past denial very quickly.

2. Anger

I have read many books and studied personal finance for many years. With all the research and reading I have done, I can confirm to you that the anger you are experiencing because of your money worries is an emotional waste of time. You are using up vital energy that should be directed at getting out of your money worries, not adding to them.

Sure, it is hard not to get angry, but where is this anger going to get you? One of my favourite pastimes is reading about, and watching old footage of, the Apollo missions to the Moon. I am fascinated by these astronauts, who really were made of the 'right stuff', but I was listening in one video to Jim Lovell, who was commander of the Apollo 13 mission, speak about the time when a hole blew in their spaceship halfway to the moon. He was asked how he reacted. Did he freak out? His answer was that they all remained very calm. He said that they could have bounced off the walls in the spaceship for twenty minutes in anger and despair, but that if they had done this, twenty minutes later there still would have been a hole in their spaceship, and what good what that have done them? So, yes, they were scared, but getting angry was not going to solve their problem, so they simply set about working out how they were going to get their spaceship back to earth. They thought rationally, what do we need to do to solve this problem? And we all know that, with the help of some engineers back at mission control, they returned safely to Earth.

So, please apply the same principles to your financial problems. You can get angry all you want, you can blame the banks for giving you the money, but you know what? *You* promised to repay them this money when they gave it to you, *you* signed the terms and conditions of the loan offer that spelled out quite clearly what would happen if you didn't pay them back, so you can get mad with them all you want, but it's not going to get you out the mess you are in.

You can also spend time beating yourself up, because after all you are the one who got yourself into this mess, right? Let's not take the pity train, OK? Let's not keep telling yourself how much of a failure you are. Listen to me: everybody fails, it's life. But you know what? You have got to learn from your failures and not repeat them ever again. Use them to your advantage, let them make you smarter, so that if there ever is a next time, you will use your experience to make much better decisions.

Here is a great quote from Denis Waitley, who said that 'Failure should be our teacher, not our undertaker. Failure is delay, not defeat. It is a temporary detour, not a dead end. Failure is something that we can avoid only by saying nothing, doing nothing, and being nothing.'

Look, of course there were situations in your past that led you to make some of the decisions that have got you into the difficulties you find yourself in today, and yes, there are external factors that you simply have no control over (if you think long and hard enough, you will find multiple circumstances, and a series of events, that led to your financial problems), but you have got to stop blaming them and everyone else, including yourself. This is your life, you are responsible and accountable for it, and if you don't face up to this, you will not be able to fix your problems, I guarantee you.

3. Depression

This is probably the worst of all the stages, and one that is very hard to control. Being in financial difficulty is not fun, and it does make us feel sad and depressed – no question about it. Not being able to repay your mortgage, not being able to find a new job, not being able to heat your home, having your home repossessed, having to give up your car for an old banger, or your partner having to go back to work are just some examples that may lead to depression.

A good friend of mine lost his job about eighteen months ago. The sector he had been successfully practising in for the last twenty years had collapsed, and it seemed that it would take at least a decade for it to recover. He didn't have that time on his side to wait around for things to recover: he had a reasonably big mortgage and other unsecured debt that had to be repaid as well. He had two months' living expenses in his bank account; once they were gone, he would have nothing.

Suffice to say, the two months came and went, and by the third month his savings were all gone. He quickly went into arrears, he couldn't get another job, he didn't want to retrain and try to reinvent himself, and he very quickly became quite depressed. He was a failure, in his own mind, to his wife and children and he just could not lift his head up from his pillow every day. Up to that point, he had been a very outgoing, extrovert type of person who would get on with anyone he met and was liked by everyone who came into contact with him, but now a cloud hung over him and he was not the same person I had known before. What made things more difficult for him was that he would not meet any of his friends because of his perceived failure. He didn't want contact with anyone, and certainly didn't want any help either.

Then one day, his wife noticed a small mark on the side of his face – a very small discolouring that she wanted him to get checked out. Of course he said no way, not because he thought it was unimportant, but because he didn't have the €60 for a GP visit. A week or two passed, and his wife, who had saved the €60, convinced him to go to his GP. Her actions saved his life because the 'spot' on the side of his face was in fact cancerous and needed immediate surgery and treatment. He had this carried out, and now he is in fine health, fully recovered.

The reason I am telling you this story is that there is a lesson to be learned: no matter how bad the situation feels, it could be worse. Even in the dark times, there are still things to be thankful for if you can try and find that rainbow rather than stare down the well.

Oddly – or maybe it isn't odd at all – it took a potentially life-threatening illness for my friend to come out of his depression. Having to survive on much less money each week isn't all that bad when you think about not being around to see your child make their Holy Communion or turn eighteen, graduate or marry. In my book, that is worse than bad, it's unthinkable.

I am a financial advisor and I am in no way qualified to speak about depression in any authoritative manner, so I won't, but I can tell you about people I know, and people I have seen, where depression literally takes possession of them. This is something you would not wish on your worst enemy. Unfortunately, money worries are making more and more people depressed. I hope that this book can be a sort of exorcism for some of them, and will help them get out of the dark place they are currently in. (By the way, medical studies show that people who think in a positive manner live longer and have fewer health problems and experience less stress than people who think in a negative manner. They get done the things that need to be done.)

If ever I start to feel worried about anything or start thinking negative thoughts, I pull the elastic band that I wear around my wrist back and let it go, and it snaps against the inside of my wrist. Suddenly my thoughts are diverted from negative thoughts to the pain I now have on my wrist. I tried this after reading about it in a book called *The One Minute Millionaire*, and you know, it actually works. It snaps you out of that thing you were thinking of that might happen in the future, and what would happen to you then, and so on. It breaks the thought cycle.

I was reading a Winnie the Pooh book to my daughter Rachel once, and there was a line in it that I always remember where Piglet turns to Winnie and asks: 'What if the tree falls on me?' Winnie simply replies: 'What if it doesn't?' No doubt everyone feels down from time to time, but with help, practice and positive thoughts, you can take control of your emotions and not let them get you down too much.

I will end this section with another quote which I think is apt for what I was just talking about: 'I, not events, have the power to make me happy or unhappy today. I can choose which it shall be. Yesterday is dead, tomorrow hasn't arrived yet. I have just one day, today, and I'm going to be happy in it.'

It comes from a very unusual source. Guess who?

Groucho Marx, of all people! What a great quote, and one you wouldn't ever attribute to him. I went looking to see if Groucho had some other profound quotes such as this one, but the best I could come up with from him was: 'One morning I shot an elephant in my pyjamas. How he got into my pyjamas I'll never know.' That's more like it!

4. Acceptance

This is the stage in your debt life-cycle where you come to terms with your problems. You are still in debt – that hasn't gone away – but you finally realise that you may not ever earn as much as you used to. Yes, you are in negative equity, and struggling to make your mortgage repayments, but hey, you are not the only one, and you know, sh*t happens!

The great thing about this stage is that you see a way out of your problems. Your exit from them may not happen overnight, but for the first time in quite a while you see your situation with great clarity and you know it is not going to be never-ending because you are going to do something about it, right? Yes, you are, and this is why you are reading this book, right? Right.

5. New Beginning
Your life will move on, and perhaps in months or maybe even years, you will start to take back control of your financial life and will begin to notice the difference.

You will have started saving again each month, you follow your spending plan each month, and one or two debts are paid off in full. Things begin to improve at work and your life begins to return to what you believe is normal. No more worries about paying the bills and no more jumping when the phone rings because you think it is the credit card company again.

This is all going to happen to you, believe me, and if you follow what I am going to show you, and make some simple and at times very hard changes to your life, I guarantee that it will.

Say it again: I am going to be debt-free.

Liam's Action List

- Write down on a sheet of paper what your greatest money worries are. Which ones do you need help with? Once you know what your worst fears are, you can develop a plan to deal with them; and once you move past denial and anger, your life will change for the better.

- If you are concerned about a particular money problem and you have been keeping it to yourself, speak to a friend or family member that you trust. Find a person you know who won't be judgemental when you tell them exactly what your money problem is. You will feel so much better telling someone else rather than bottling it all up.

- When you are having money problems, it is very easy to take all the blame yourself. You may look back at decisions you made and think, 'How stupid could I have been? And look what this is doing to my family.' Please don't do this – it will get you nowhere. What's done is done, keep your eyes on the future and bear in mind that your self-worth is not dependent on your net-worth. There is nothing constructive about comparing what you had in the past to what you have right now.

- Write down five things in your life that you used to think were important, but have since discovered that, after experiencing financially difficulty, aren't important anymore. These could be physical things like expensive cars, second properties and so on. They could also be qualities like status, titles or what other people think of you.

- Write down what is most important to you now.

- Find out if there are support groups in your area. Do you know others who need financial guidance and help like you do? If there isn't, maybe you could form an informal club for people with money concerns. Talking with people who can relate to your situation is comforting and empowering. And every person will have different strengths and bring different ideas to the group.

- Be positive! Having an upbeat attitude will help you succeed. It has been proven that a person living with a positive state of mind generally goes farther in just about everything they do. Surrounding yourself with positive people will also help you succeed.

'Today, there are three kinds of people: the haves, the have-nots, and the have-not-paid-for-what-they-haves.'

–Earl Wilson

03

The 'Debtictionary' of Getting Out of Debt

There are some fundamental rules that you need to be familiar with if you want to get out of debt. These rules are not an industry secret; they are well known and well documented.

Of course the problem is that most people do not know what these rules are, but I am going to tell you them now, so you have an immediate advantage over most other people who are in debt because they have no clue (and nor does their financial advisor), believe me. Because of this lack of knowledge, people move from fear to anger, from denial to giving up, and from being motivated back to fear, all the time, and they get into this vicious circle that gets them absolutely nowhere.

I have put together a 'debtictionary' for you because I think it is very important that you gain these insights into how you begin to deal with your debt, and how you can react to and deal with your situation.

A = Action

You know the old saying about how on earth could you eat an elephant, it is so big? The answer, of course, is that you start off by eating small amounts. The same applies to debt. Many people look at their overall level of debt and don't know where to start.

They think that it is far too big for them to tackle. So what do they do? Absolutely nothing. If you decide to do this, if *you* choose this course, your debts will follow you forever and your life will be incredibly unfulfilling and unpleasant.

I think that we get one chance on this earth, so let's make the most of it. I absolutely understand that some days will be better than others, but you have got to take action and put a plan in place that you are going to stick to if you want to rid yourself of this debt. You have got to make decisions, you have got to meet your creditors, you have got to make sacrifices, and you have got to make agreements and stick to them.

As someone once said to me: before you can fight, you have to turn up in the ring.

B = Budget

Before you can start to improve your finances, you need to know exactly what you are up against and what you need to change. Adding 10 percent to 'I don't know' or taking 50 percent away from 'I haven't a clue' makes no sense at all.

So, you need to analyse your income and outgoings each month. I am going to help you with this. For many people, this is not going to be a fun process, but taking responsibility rarely is. However, it is necessary if you want to improve your finances.

Just remember that a little pain now will result in a lot of pleasure and financial freedom down the road. By the way, a budget is just a plan – a plan for where you want your money to go. It's based on how much you make and how much you spend each month. It ensures that you have money available to cover your expenses and that you are not spending more than you absolutely need to. It also highlights areas that you are not spending enough of your money on. I want people to spend money on things they get enjoyment from, so if that means spending a lot of money on a gym membership, for example, then great, but don't spend your money on things you don't like or don't use. A budget will help you achieve this.

Don't you think it makes sense that you should spend some time each month making sure you are getting the most of the cash you spend most of your time working to earn each month? I do.

C = Co-operation

You will not be able to resolve your debt problems without the help of your creditors, so you have to reach agreements with them, and work together to arrive at a solution that you are both happy with.

I know this is easier said than done, because sometimes your creditors can be completely unreasonable when you are being very reasonable, and this can be a perceived stumbling block for you. I have found that at the first sign that your creditor is unwilling to work with you or agree to what you have proposed to them, people tend to throw in the towel. Don't give up. Yes, you might be – and in some cases probably are – dealing with a bunch of morons, but if your proposal is logical, practical and makes sense to them and you, stick to your guns and take control of the situation yourself.

Before you do this, exhaust all efforts with your creditor first. There might be a Plan A, a Plan B and even a Plan C before you both arrive at a compromise you are happy with, so try and work with your creditor and not against them. Don't forget, they hold the power, not you, so find common ground that is acceptable to you both. One quick word of caution: don't over-promise in order to arrive at an agreement. Be honest with them, because once you come to an agreement you have got to stick to it!

D = Debt Collectors

If debt collectors are calling you, try and reason with them. I realise that this will be hard. They have probably spent the whole day being hung up on, cursed at and insulted by others, so don't expect that they will be in a good mood when they speak with you. Count on the fact that some will be nasty because they are under enormous pressure to collect as much as they can, as quickly as they can.

However, you can use debt collectors to your advantage. If you do not pay your debt for one reason or another, eventually it will enter the collections process. In most cases, your debt will be sold to a debt collection agency – at an enormous discount to the collection agent. In some cases, discounts can be as high as 90 percent. This means that your creditor, in order to recoup some money, may sell your €1,000 debt for as little as €100.

Now remember, debt collection agencies are companies that are looking to make a profit. They are out to make money. But be aware that these companies, as I have just said, buy debts for cents on the euro. Knowing this fact can often give you the courage to make settlement offers you would otherwise be too shy to make, or may think are far too low.

Here is a great tip: if you are going to make an offer to a debt collection agency for the settlement of your debt, wait until the last few days of the month. They will have quotas and will want to make sure that they recover as much as they can each month. Their representatives are under pressure to meet goals and targets, and you can use this against them.

Call them on the last day of the month and make your offer. They may hesitate at first, but stick to your guns. A client of mine owed €3,500 to a credit card company and at the end of

December he made an offer to them of €450 for full settlement of his account. Guess what? They accepted it!

E = Energy

You will need to keep your energy levels as high as you can. Staying fit and healthy both physically and mentally is very important. A healthy body will help you stay focused and determined. It is a scientific fact that when you feel physically well, you have more energy to tackle your problems.

Getting out of debt takes a huge amount of effort, and if you are mentally and physically not in the best shape, then all this effort will be difficult to find, and you will get nowhere.

Go for that walk, run or cycle. Clear your head for thirty minutes each day. Forget about your worries if you can – it's amazing that when times you are not thinking about your money worries, and obsessing about trying to find an answer to them, out of the blue something will pop into your head that you'd never thought about, or an idea for a new business may suddenly appear out of nowhere. It is hard to get these inspirational moments sitting at home reading the newspaper – which is full of doom and gloom anyway – and you are not going to get inspired watching *Deal or No Deal*, so get out of the house for thirty minutes each day. It is good to have 'me time'; it will do you a world of good.

F = Fear

There are so many things we could be afraid of, aren't there? But you know, fear robs us of rational thought, and of the ability to approach things in a calm and logical manner. Fear clouds our judgement as well and makes us focus on the next twenty-four hours rather than the next twenty-four months.

I was working with a company that was going through a redundancy programme. They asked me to come in and help their staff with some of the financial issues and concerns they might have, before and after they left their current job.

So, I began by asking them what their fears were. Some said not being able to get another job, others not being able to pay their mortgage, others that they might be bored being at home all of the time. There are many things that people facing redundancy get worried about.

Of course, nine times out of ten the biggest fear is related to money. Fear grips people and makes them think that their house, for example, is going to be repossessed. Because of this fear, they do stupid things like paying a lump sum off their mortgage with some of their redundancy money.

Let me show you an example of this. I met a guy who recently received about €45,000 net from a redundancy payment from his former employer. He was fearful that he would get into arrears on his mortgage, so the next day he went into his bank and took €30,000 off the amount he owed on his mortgage. This left him with €15,000.

Three weeks later, he received a letter from his bank saying, in effect: thank you very much for that €30,000, and now, in return, your monthly repayment has reduced by a whopping €72 each month! Fear had made this guy do something insane. He was worried about his mortgage, and thought that by taking €30,000 off the amount he owed, he would somehow be protected from having his house repossessed if he didn't get a job in the near future.

But what would have been better for this guy? A higher balance outstanding with a mortgage repayment he could afford, because he could have put away €20,000 into a dedicated 'mortgage account' that would have paid his mortgage for the next two years if he didn't find a job? Or a lower balance with a revised repayment that he still can't afford, which puts huge pressure on him to find a job – any job – as quickly as possible?

He should have been putting all his time and energy into finding a new job, a new career, without having to worry about his mortgage – which would have been fine anyway. This should have been an opportunity for him to reinvent himself. Instead, fear threatened his security. When we feel that our security is under threat, we make irrational and emotional decisions that, in the cold light of day, we regret having made.

G = Gambling

Earlier this year, I was doing a TV programme on this topic and was talking about how I have encountered people who engage in gambling as a last-ditch effort to save themselves from financial ruin.

I have *never* come across anyone who has solved their financial problems by gambling. However, I have come across plenty of people who added to their debts and problems when they started gambling.

Your odds of winning are terrible, and when I tell people that if they buy more Lottery tickets, for example, your chances of winning don't increase dramatically if you buy five tickets instead of one. If you like playing the Lottery for fun or you like an occasional bet on the 'gee-gees', then great, but don't think that this is going to be your way out of debt.

The topic of gambling obviously hit a nerve, because the number of calls and emails I received from viewers following that TV programme amazed even me. The number of stories from people telling me what happened to them and their family because of gambling was truly heartbreaking. As they say, you don't know what goes on behind closed doors.

One letter I received, from a lady in the midlands, told me about her situation and how her husband had lost a lot of their money, unknown to her, through gambling. His gambling started off small but gradually built up over the years to fairly high levels. He remortgaged their house to raise money so that he could place bets – which, he hoped, would win him enough money to allow him to clear the mortgage off in full! Of course he ended up losing it all and still had a huge mortgage. When his income was reduced in the downturn, he could not meet his mortgage repayments and they went into arrears.

Gambling eventually took this man's life. One day, when she returned home after collecting their two young kids from school, she found him hanging in the garden shed. He thought that his death would improve his wife and his children's lives; he thought that he would never be able to stop gambling and that the only way out was to take his own life. Their lives have not improved one bit, however: two young children now don't have a dad, one young wife doesn't have a husband, two parents don't have a son, and so on.

Don't let gambling take hold of you, and don't think for a second that it is going to solve your money problems. It won't. Please get professional help for your problem.

H = Help

This is an area of concern for me because I still see people who lack the required 'know-how' and yet try to solve their problems on their own. This can be a mistake because many people make decisions based on opinions and hearsay rather than facts. Of course, the reason they don't look for help in the first place is possibly because of embarrassment, due to their fear that people will think they are stupid, or because they believe that their situation is beyond recovery.

Yes, there are some things that I am sure you are more than capable of doing on your own, but don't bury your head in the sand: seek help from qualified professional advisors – preferably ones who are not going to charge you a fee. MABS are a useful resource, and one that many people turn to when they need help. I would encourage you to get help from people who have expertise in this area. Their advice and help could make all the difference to you.

A word of caution: there are a lot of financial predators out there who are like vultures, preying on, and benefiting from, other people's misfortunes. They use your vulnerability to take money from you each month by promising to act on your behalf and deal with your creditors for you. They will charge you an upfront fee and take a monthly charge for themselves – money which could be used to reduce your debts.

I came across a man who was about to use the service of a debt advisory firm. The firm was going to charge him an upfront fee of €500 and a monthly fee of €75 for the next five years. In total, he was going to pay them €5,000. I acted on his behalf instead: I wrote two letters and made two phone calls, and the problem was sorted out. No need for €5,000 – no need for any money, in fact. So use the services of MABS or free advisory agencies, and don't *ever* pay for this type of service.

I = Interest

I was working with a company recently giving financial seminars to their staff members. I carried out a financial awareness questionnaire with them where one of the questions I posed was: 'Do you know how much your loan (or loans) are costing you in interest each month?' Astonishingly, 87 percent of the respondents had absolutely no idea how much they were paying in interest each month.

I am going to show you why you really need to sit up and take notice of interest, whether it is the amount you earn on your savings or the amount it is costing you in loans.

When asked to name the greatest invention in human history, Albert Einstein simply replied 'compound interest'. He went on by saying that 'compound interest is the eighth wonder of the world. He who understands it, earns it. He who doesn't, pays it.'

Let's look at how interest can end up costing you a fortune if you do not take any notice of it, and what you can do to prevent this from happening in the future.

The single biggest indication that the loan you are paying is a bad one is if the interest rate is high. For example, let's assume that you borrow €1,000 over a four-year period at 18 percent. In that time, this loan will cost you €410 in interest over the term of the loan. In my book, that's an interest rate of 41 percent, or nearly half of the amount you borrowed, in interest alone.

Here's an old favourite: the interest rate charged on your credit card, and what it will end up costing you if you just pay the minimum amount due each month. Let me give you two examples of how an interest rate could cripple you financially if you let it, and how you can overcome it. But before I do this, let me first show you the impact that interest rates, and paying the minimum amount each month on your credit card, can have on your finances. Let's assume that you buy the following items and pay the minimum amount each month on a card charging you 16 percent:

- If you bought a computer for €1,500 and paid the minimum amount each month, it will take you *18 years 8 months* to pay it off in full, and it will cost you €1,492 in interest payments.

- If you had a debt of €10,000 at 16 percent and you paid the minimum each month, it will take you *31 years 11 months* to repay in full – and €10,713 in interest payments in the process.

Let me give you another example of how being aware of interest and how it applies to your loan can save you thousands in interest payments.

Let's assume that you borrow €200,000 to buy a house at 4 percent interest over a thirty-year period. Your monthly repayment is going to be €954, and the amount of interest you are going to repay over that thirty-year term is €143,739.

If you borrowed the same €200,000 at the same rate (4 percent), but this time over a twenty-year period, your monthly repayment would be €1,211, and the overall interest you would pay is €90,870.

So, for the sake of an extra €260 each month, you will save yourself €53,000 in interest payments.

OK, let's talk about interest and the impact it can have on your savings.

Let me start off with a very quick factual statement: if you saved €100 per month at the age of twenty, when you reach the age of sixty-five you would be a millionaire. When people say to me that they will never be able to save a million euro in their lifetime, I love to tell them this fact. I ask them would they be able to save €1 per day. Of course the answer is yes, they could have, but they never did, and now they think it is too late. It might be too late for some to save a million at one euro per day, but that doesn't mean you shouldn't start. You might not reach a million, but you might accumulate a tidy sum nonetheless, so let the magic of compound interest work its magic.

Here's another example of how saving early and letting the interest you earn make more interest. If I saved €100 per month when I was twenty-five for just ten years, at a 7 percent return each year, I would have €135,045 in my account at age sixty-five. If I was thirty-five years old and saved €100 each month but this time I saved it for thity years, I would have €121,287 in my account. So, even though I saved for three times as long, I would be behind by €15,000.

Finally, here is a great example of how interest rates can work for and against you. If you owed €3,000 at 18 percent per annum, in year ten you would owe €15,701. On the other hand, if you had that same €3,000 on deposit earning a reasonable rate each year, you would have around €9,317 in your account. Can you see how it can work for and against you?

I hope that I have showed you, with some of these examples, that having the right information and knowledge to hand when it comes to interest and how it can work for and against you can have a major impact on your financial well-being. You need to keep yourself informed, educate yourself and become aware of your finances.

J = Job

There are two ways you can get rid of your debt: either reduce your outgoings or increase your income. Obviously the job market is very tough at the moment, and getting a job is very difficult, to say the least.

But you have to make a job of getting a job, which means using your network of friends and family, updating your CV, identifying potential new employers, retraining, setting up your own business, and so on.

Don't take the easy way out by just sending out your CV and waiting for a response. The likelihood is that you won't even get one. If you want a job, go out and get it: create it, fight for it, go after it.

No job is beneath you. I still run into people who refuse to take some jobs because they see it as 'beneath them'. Some people feel that other people would think less of them if they did the work. I assure you that people won't – and to hell with them if they do.

Be courageous and get the job you want – or the job you need, at the very least. It will help with the bills for now, until you can find something better.

K = Knowledge

In his book *Rich Dad Poor Dad*, author Robert Kiyosaki says that without education and information, you cannot transform either into useful knowledge that can be acted upon in your best interests. So you have got to find out as much as you possibly can about what you need to do in order to get out of the situation you find yourself in. You need to educate yourself in these matters – or have someone do it for you. Luckily for you, by reading this book you are getting both.

L = Language

Much like beliefs, words can bring us up or tear us down. When it comes to finances, the words we use to describe who we are, what we want, or what holds us back can have a huge impact, positive or negative. Very often the words you use to describe your financial condition will *become* your financial condition. So, choose your words wisely. Over the years, I've heard a number of phrases used by people when they are asked how they are doing financially, such as: getting by, hanging in there, holding it together, robbing Peter to pay Paul, making ends meet, and so on. I know it is tough, but remember, you are what you say, so speak powerfully, positively, and with a vision of how you want things to be.

M = Money

Look, money is not the root of all evil – which is a common misconception people have. Neither is money only for those who are greedy and wealthy. Money is nothing more than pieces of paper that are used as a unit of exchange. Of course we need it to survive and keep a roof over our heads, and food on the table, but when you think of money, think of it as nothing more than ink on paper.

Money is not the problem if you are working in a job you dislike, and it is not the problem if your employer is not paying you enough for the job you are doing. It is not why you are in debt either: it was just what you used to get yourself there in the first place.

N = Now

If you want to get your finances back on track, there is no time like the present, so you need to get motivated, get that belief, and get started on a plan *now*. Don't wait for things to happen, like your bank magically taking thousands of euro off your debt. It won't happen. You have got to take back control of your finances and take action in the areas where you have control. But don't give me the 'I'll start tomorrow' or 'Once I have this lined up' or 'When this thing happens' I will get started. It won't happen! Don't kid yourself. You know deep down that you are just putting it off, for whatever reason. When I agreed to write this book, it was, believe me, a daunting project and a huge commitment in terms of my time and effort. Many times I would say to myself 'I must start the book tonight' – or tomorrow, or whenever – and I could always come up with any number of excuses if I wanted to, and never get around to actually doing anything. Of course when you then have to do it, the pressure is on. You don't have time on your side, and you rush things, and then you wonder why things didn't turn out as you had planned.

Don't put things off: act *now*, put together a timeline of events, and plan what needs to be done and when it has to be achieved. You can have all the passion and determination in the world, but if you don't act now, you will just be wasting your time and energy.

O = Opportunity

Many people who are in debt because they were made redundant feel that they may never get another job. Some fail to see that losing their job could in fact be an opportunity to reinvent themselves and make changes to their life that they never would have done if they had stayed in their previous job.

People who have been made redundant have two choices: they can feel sorry for themselves and put the position they find themselves in down to events beyond their control. For many this is a reasonable argument. But for others, redundancy might just be the jumpstart they need to help them seek out new opportunities and challenges and pursue dreams and passions they never dared try until now because they are saying to themselves in a positive way, *what have I got to lose?*

The majority of people would rather live within their means than expand their realities. Let me explain what I mean by this. People are more comfortable working hard all their lives than being temporarily uncomfortable in order to change their lives and the way they think. Using the metaphor of switching from right hand to left hand, most people would rather be poor eating with their right hand forever, than become rich by learning to eat with their left. In many ways, what is required at this moment in time is a change in mentality.

P = Patience

You are certainly going to need plenty of patience as you work your way out of debt: patience with yourself, your partner, and especially your creditors. But stick with it: it will be worth it in the long run.

You are also going to need patience in relation to your spending habits. You need to make sure you don't impulse-buy, you need to use cash instead of your credit card, and you need to plan your spending well in advance and only buy what you need, rather than what you want. This is easier said than done, but if you can train yourself to be patient, the delayed gratification will be worth the wait, I assure you.

Q = Questions

In his best-selling book *Awaken the Giant Within*, Tony Robbins devoted an entire chapter to the importance of asking good questions. He said: 'If you want to have a better quality of life, ask a better question.'

Start by asking yourself some of the following questions:

- Did I consider the cost of borrowing and how it will affect my overall financial plan?
- Do I need this item, or is it something I want but can do without?
- Would I be better off investing the money I would be paying in interest?
- Where is this money coming from? Have I earned it, or do I still have to work for it?
- Did I consider how much I can save if I save the money first, then come back next year and buy it for cash?

Before purchasing something, wealthy people ask themselves these types of questions to help them focus on the total cost or the consequences of their actions.

R = Responsibility

Make sure that you are not the only member of your household taking responsibility for your finances, and taking action in this area. If you are working hard at saving money and getting out of debt but your spouse is out spending as if there was no tomorrow, you are fighting a losing battle.

Sit down together and make a plan to determine how much spending money you each should have, then check in at the end of the week to see how well you are doing. It still amazes me how many people operate separate bank accounts. Myself and Roseann operate one account and have done since we got married. We both know exactly how much is in it at any given time. We know how much we can spend each month, what date direct debits are coming out, and so on. I still come across couples who are married or living together but whose finances are 'living apart'. This is not a good place to be. Don't hide savings or debt from your partner: let them know exactly what you have, where it is and how much you owe. If you plan to spend money on a luxury item, sit down with them, talk about it, and involve them in the decision, as it affects them as well.

If the entire family shares the responsibility for your monthly budget, for example, and everyone can cut back a little bit, it will make a big difference.

One person should not have to shoulder the entire debt burden of the household. Remember the old saying: two heads are better than one.

S = Savings

Whenever I meet people to go through their income and outgoings, I almost always notice that they never include savings as an expense. The response I always get is that savings isn't an expense – and then they tell me that there is normally nothing left at the end of the month to save, and that is why they don't save.

First of all, savings *is* an expense – and that is how you have to treat it. It should be as important as paying your mortgage or your electricity bill each month. In other words, a certain amount should go out of your account into a dedicated savings account – end of story.

Secondly, do not wait until the end of the month to save whatever is left over. Plan your spending before the month starts, and know exactly what you have set aside for food, clothing, utilities and so on before you even get paid. Don't 'wing it', otherwise you will, I guarantee, run out of money before the month is over.

So, let me say this again: plan your spending before the month begins, and then you won't have to analyse what went wrong at the end of the month.

I am sure you're thinking: 'How can I save money when my outgoings exceed what I earn? I can't even pay my mortgage, and he wants me to start saving money.' Yes, that is absolutely correct: even if you are in that situation, I want you to start saving. And you know what? It isn't the amount that's important, it's getting into the habit of saving and building up for a reserve so that (a) you will feel better about yourself when you see that there is some money in your account, and (b) you will have savings to fall back on should you need funds in an emergency. Having savings that you can call on prevents you from having to get further into debt in the future!

Some people make the mistake, when dealing with creditors, of thinking that they cannot put down on their financial statement that they are saving money each month. They think that their creditor will frown upon this – and in some cases they will. They will want your money all for themselves, and will try and bully you into giving it to them. Under no circumstances should you allow this to happen. Make sure you include savings in your get-out-of-debt plan, because it is an integral part of that plan.

Start off slowly. It is recommended that you save 10 percent of your net monthly income, but if you can't do this, why not start with 1 percent? If your household income is €3,000 per month, do you think you could find €30 each month? Could you not find €1 per day? I guarantee you that if you do this, you won't have €365 at the end of the year, you will have more, because money will be attracted to you. You will save another €10 here and there from a refund or a gift; you will save some money by bringing your lunch to work a day or two each week, and so on.

Then, after a year, you may be able to increase your 1 percent to 2 percent, and then, in another six months' time you might even manage to save 3 percent of your salary. The key is to start, and make saving automatic. If your employer can deduct money at source from your salary each month, then all the better, because you will never see it – and you will never be tempted to spend it.

T = Time

Getting out of debt will take time, and it is important that you approach the process with this mentality. You have to take it one day at a time; there is no quick fix to your problems. But you have to set yourself some goals, for instance that you will be debt-free at a particular point in the future. You have to set yourself a time goal that you will have a certain amount of debt cleared in a certain number of months or years. Without this measurable goal, you will have no idea how well – or how badly – you are doing.

If you want to run a marathon, you can't immediately go out and run one. You need time to train, to get your body into shape, so that if you follow a certain training schedule, over time you will get into shape, and you will be able to run 26.1 miles. The same applies to your finances: you need time, you need to be realistic, and you need to train your mind to achieve your goals.

U = Unnecessary

If you look closely enough at your monthly outgoings, you will find that many of the costs you are incurring each month are absolutely unnecessary. Many of these costs may be quite small, but some could be very large amounts. For example, many people are paying about €50 more each month than they need to for movie or sports channels they don't watch. If you watch these channels, then fine, you are getting value for your money, but if you don't, then why continue to pay the subscription? Let me give you an example of this relating to a couple I came across recently. He liked golf, and the Ryder Cup was on TV so he subscribed to the relevant sports channel for a month so that he could watch this event. It cost him about an extra €50 for the month, but it was worth it. The Ryder Cup came and went, but this guy forgot to call the TV company to cancel his subscription. Four months later, he is still paying an extra €50 per month; in other words, he has now paid €200 more than he needed to.

Another completely unnecessary expense is the late fees and the over-the-limit fees your bank and credit card company hits you with each month. A client of mine was paying €100 each month towards her credit card debt, but she was paying it about a week later than she was supposed to, so she was hit with a €15 late payment fee each month. Over the course of two years, she had paid €360 in late payment fees, as well as interest of 20 percent on the credit card borrowing itself. It is predicted that the credit card industry will make in excess of 20 billion euro in late fees and penalties this year worldwide.

To get over the problem of late fees, I contacted her credit card provider and asked them to amend her repayment date, and they said they would do so. A thirty-second phone call saved this women €180 a year in unnecessary fees.

People also often pay far too much for life assurance each month. Of course, if you arrange your policy via a broker, who gets paid commission for arranging the insurance for you from a life assurance company, it might be in their best interests that you pay as much as possible. I recently met a couple who were paying €394.15 per month for a mortgage protection policy. And do you know what they should have been paying? Just €66.78 per month. In other words, they were paying an extra €327.37 per month, or €3,928.44 over the course of a year – and a whopping €98,211 – over the term of the policy. (Of course, some brokers recommend, and arrange, the best product for you regardless of what they get paid.)

V = Vision

I really like the TV show *The Mentalist*. There are some episodes where Patrick Jane (the central character) comes up against a guy called Bret Stiles (played by Malcolm McDowell), the leader of a cult called the Visualize Self-Realisation Centre.

Whenever I see these episodes, I begin to think about my finances ten years ago: if I hadn't started visualising what I wanted to become, it would never have happened. So let me be a bit of a Bret Stiles for a moment.

Find a quite location where you can be by yourself for twenty minutes. Close your eyes, sit back and think about what your life would be like if you didn't have all of these debts? What would it be like if you were not in negative equity? What would your relationships be like with your partner, your family, your friends, your work colleagues, your neighbours? Would you be happier?

If the vision that you begin to create in your mind is what you truly want to have, then make it the foundation for everything you have to do to get out of debt. Commit to doing everything that supports this vision, and regularly spend twenty minutes visualising what it would be like to be debt-free.

I did, and so did many thousands of others I have helped over the past twenty years. It really does work.

W = Wants

I am sure that with all the loans you have, you could look at each one and give me a reason why you took it out in the first place. You will tell me that each of them was needed at the particular time when you took it out.

Let me tell you a few home truths. Most of the short-term debt we accumulate is not because we needed the money for something, it is because we *wanted* the money for something.

When I met a young couple recently and was going through their finances, I asked them to explain what their €8,000 debt to their credit union was for, their reply was that they had used the money on their back garden. They continued that they had used the money to install artificial grass, new decking, and a new play area and swings for their kids. With the balance, they went on a foreign holiday for two weeks. Can you believe it: borrowing money to put down artificial grass for a three-bedroom, semi-detached house?

So, let's admit something here: on occasion we borrow money for things we want rather than things we need. In finance, there is a huge difference between needs and wants, and you need to understand this difference if you want to get control over your borrowing habits.

Let me give you an example. You may need a car to get you to and from work: it is a necessity. But then you start thinking about the type of car you want, and this starts to override your need. You now want a new car, you want it in a certain colour, and you want a certain model, so you borrow €20,000 to buy it – without fully considering the consequences.

Stop borrowing money for things you *want* to have. If you want it badly enough, save the cash and then buy it. A loan for a car takes four or five years to pay back. Do you have a savings account with enough money in it to cover unforeseen events that may occur during those years? What is the point of having a car for which you are paying a fortune each month, when you could be two pay cheques away from financial disaster if you lost your job?

Y = Year

Make this the year that you commit to getting out of debt, and start actually getting out of debt. You are going to look back in years to come on this year, as the one when you chose to regain control of your financial life. After reading this book, you are going to know the precise month and year when you are going to be financially free from the debt that is currently weighing you down. And that is really something to look forward to.

Z = Zero

This is the ultimate number you are aiming for. Don't aim for anything else. Don't settle for being €10,000 in debt, or €1,000 in debt. Aim to be beholden to no one, and make your target number zero. You are going to owe nothing, nada, zip, zero – and don't settle for anything less.

Liam's Action List

- Get some exercise. Exercise is a great and proven method of creating energy that helps you think better and more clearly. Do something that will get your heart pumping for ten minutes every day.

- Decide that today you are going to take care of one financial issue that has been bothering you. It may be returning a call to your mortgage lender or it may be contacting your credit card company about your arrears.

- Resolve to practice one good money habit this week. It might be bringing lunch to work, not using your credit card this week, setting a budget or recording where you spend your money and on what this week. And make that practice part of your financial life – not just for this week, but for the other fifty-one as well.

- Start educating yourself about financial issues. The more information you have at your disposal the better, and your finances will only improve if you get yourself up to speed. Many people find financial topics complicated, so they just switch off and let others make decisions for them. Don't let this happen to you! If you are not involved in your own plan, chances are you will fall into someone else's.

- Start putting together a timeline of what needs to be done, by whom, and when it is realistically going to be completed.

- Make a list of tasks and make sure that you do everything you ask yourself to do.

- Your finances aren't going to improve overnight, so don't get discouraged if you don't see immediate results. It will take time, but you need to know what your 'Debt-Free Day' is going to be. It might be five years away, it might be ten, but it is important to have something to work towards.

- It may take time to learn how to identify ways to avoid getting into financial difficulty, but try to get into the habit of tackling problems before they even arise.

- Keep an eye on those small things, especially if you think they will not have a major impact on your overall finances. You need to be diligent and follow through on the tasks and goals you promised to keep. Those small little things, like just paying minimum payments on your credit card bill, can quickly add up to a big mess if you don't take care of them in a timely and efficient manner.

'Christmas is the season when you buy this year's gifts with next year's money.'

–**Unknown**

04

Assessing Your Situation

Given that you have this book in your hand, I am assuming that you have a problem with your finances. You either have lots of debt, or you have little or no savings, or maybe it is a combination of both. This book is going to help you with both of these problems.

Your current financial situation is a direct reflection of your inner relationship with money. If you don't like the current state of your finances, something needs to change in that relationship.

If you have a problem with money and debt, how can you solve it if you don't know what you are up against? Without accurate, up-to-date information, it is impossible to create an accurate picture of your financial situation. If you don't know where your money goes each month, you will have no idea where you stand, what needs to be improved, and which areas you are doing well at.

Easier said than done, I hear you say. I know that one of the most difficult things for anyone to do is to track their spending. To write down every little thing you spend money on is very difficult. Why? Well, most of us simply don't want to know: we are aware that the news is going to be bad.

But let me tell you this: not wanting to know will only get you further into trouble than you aready are. If you want to improve your finances and get different results, you need to change your behaviour. This starts with being honest about what is going on each month. You have to look at the facts and not flinch.

If you want to become debt-free, you have to be realistic and honest about your financial situation. You need to track your spending. The truth will set you free, I assure you, but it is a pain in the arse in the meantime.

Financial Awareness Quiz

Our starting point is to see how much you know about your own finances. Time to get out a pen and paper. I am going to ask you some questions, and I want you to answer them honestly and to the best of your ability. When you sit down to review your answers, they will tell you a lot about your knowledge of your finances and will raise some very interesting issues, which we will be work on throughout the book. This quiz is to help you focus on your finances and get your head into the right space.

Money Management

- How much do you spend on average each week?
- Do you prefer to use cash or cards?
- What luxuries do you buy each day, and each week? Include newspapers, coffees, lunch and so on.
- What do you spend most of your money on?
- Do you have a monthly budget?
- How often do you use the ATM each week?
- Are you concerned about your spending each week?

Debt

- How much money do you owe?

- Who do you owe this money to?

- What do you owe this money for? Are you paying for cars, education, past holidays?

- How much do you pay in interest each month?

- What are the interest rates on each of your loans, and on each of your credit cards?

- Are any of your bills past their due-by date?

- Do you ever pay late fees or overdraft fees? If yes, how often?

- Do you receive letters from collection agencies or creditors?

- Have you ever received a phone call at home from one of your creditors?

- What balance are you carrying on your credit card?

- Do you pay the full amount due each month, or just the minimum payment?

- What percentage of available credit are you using? For example, if you have a balance of €50 and a limit of €500, you are using 10 percent of your credit.

- Do you worry about your debts? Do you lose sleep thinking about them?

Expenses

- How much are your fixed and variable expenses each month?

- How much do you spend on food, loans and utilities?

- How much do you spend on nonessential items such as movie and sports channels, gym membership, takeaways and so on?

- Do your find that your expenses vary from month to month?

- If you lost your primary source of income, how much money would you need to have to live the way you currently do for six months?

- Do you have a car? How much does it cost you to run it each month? Include loan repayments, insurance, tax and fuel.

- If you could use public transport to get to work, how much would this cost you?

Savings

- How much do you have in total in savings?

- How much do you save each month?

- Where do you keep your savings?

- When was the last time you dipped into your savings?

- Why did you have to dip into them?

- How long would your savings support you if you lost your job?

- How much have you saved for retirement? Do you know what the monthly old-age pension is?

- How much do you think you need to save for retirement?

- Do you think you are saving enough?

- If you died, do you know how much your partner would receive from lump sum payments, pension, and so on?

Banking

- Do you have a bank account?

- Are your accounts in good standing, with positive balances?

- What type of account do you have?

- What interest rate is paid on these accounts?

- What monthly fees does your account attract?

- Have you been in overdraft recently?

- Have you ever missed a loan repayment or any direct debits from your account because of having 'insufficient funds'?

Income

- In the last tax year, what was your income?

- How much do you earn each week/month?

- How much more would you like to earn this year? Put a figure on it.

- How do you plan to earn this money? Being promoted? Doing overtime? Taking on a second job? Going into further education? Embarking on a new career? Starting a business?

- Are you happy with your current job?

Investment

- Do you know what a stock, bond or managed fund is?

- Have you ever invested before?

- If you have, how have your investments performed over the course of a year? Have they gained or lost value? Include the value of your pension when answering this question.

- How much money have you invested? Approximate figures will suffice.

- What have you invested your money in?

- Do you have an emergency fund? If so, how much is in it?

- Do you know what you are being charged each month in fees for your investment account?

- What was the last financial or business news article you read?

- Do you know what your current/previous pension contribution is invested in each month?

- Do you regularly take notice of how your pension is performing?

- Do you think you are investing enough?

Whenever I get people to carry out this exercise, the majority have no idea what the answers are to most of the questions. So if this happened to you, then relax: you are perfectly normal. Some of the questions are difficult to answer without first looking up bank statements, but you should be able to answer the majority of the questions. Not knowing the answers is one of the reasons your finances are not in as good a state as you would like them to be.

Each question is directly linked to the others, and each will have a big impact on other area. So this quiz was just for starters: it was designed to get you into that uncomfortable place and ask you those questions that you ought to know the answers to, but don't. We are going to start working on this now so that when you take the quiz again, at the end of the book, you will know the answer to every question.

Where are you now?

The next thing we have to do is analyse your monthly income and outgoings. Let me give you a quick heads-up before we start this section: this is not going to be a fun process, but it is a necessary step in looking after and improving your finances. Just remember, a little pain now will result in a lot of pleasure and financial freedom in the not-too-distant future.

Let me again use the example of losing weight and improving your health. I believe that people who set out to lose weight with the intention of keeping it off start by making a honest assessment of their current weight and health condition. Based on where they are now, they create a clear vision of what weight they want to reach, how they want to feel, and what they want to look like in the future. They do this by assessing where they are right now and then building a plan that sets them up for long-lasting success – in contrast with someone who is just going on a diet.

The same principles apply to your finances. Let's find out what state your finances are in right now, down to the last cent, and then let's put a plan in place to improve them.

If you set out to travel to a particular destination, how would you get there? How would you know where to go? Of course it depends on where you start from, but you won't be able to go anywhere until you know where you currently are. This is the taking-stock process. So let's get cracking on your numbers.

Step 1

What I want you to do here is list all of the assets you currently have. Here is a table with some suggestions for you:

Description	Value
Savings account	
Investment account	
Life insurance (only policies that have some cash value, not death benefits)	
Equity investment property	
Equity in your own home	
Education/children's savings accounts	
Car(s)	
Household items (computers, bikes, heirlooms)	
Jewellery	
Any other assets of value	

The purpose of this exercise is to get a snapshot of where your finances are at this point in time. It's simple enough: subtract everything you owe from everything you own that has value. If you owe more than you own, you are in the red, but regardless of whether you are in the red or the black, at least we've put a figure on it. Later on in the book, I will show you how to increase your net worth.

I think this is a great exercise to carry out, partly because it will show you if your assets and liabilities actually stack up. Let me explain this a little: in the days of the 'Celtic Tiger', people were preparing net-worth statements in order to secure a particular loan. However, they ended up overvaluing their assets. If someone had taken the time to analyse the net-worth statements, they may not have over-borrowed.

For example, when you carry out this exercise, I want you to take a close look at your assets. Are they in short-term deposit accounts while all your loans are long-term ones? Do you owe more in mortgages than the properties are worth? We will be able to correct these mismatches as we proceed. The important thing at this stage is to record them, so that we can identify them.

After drawing up your net-worth statement, you should revisit it from time to time. As you increase your savings and pay off debt, your net worth will grow – and you will become even more motivated to increase it further. For the time being, though, let's look at your current net worth.

Step 2
This is where I want you to look at everything you owe, the amount outstanding, the term remaining and so on. To help you with this, I have another table for you to fill in!

Description of debt	Balance outstanding	Term remaining	Monthly Repayment	Interest Rate Charged
Mortgage				
Mortgage No. 2				
Personal loan				
Personal loan No. 2				
Credit Card				
Credit Union				
Business loan				
Loans from family/ friends				
Any other debt owing (Revenue, property tax etc.)				

Step 3
Here I want you to look at your net monthly income and your total outgoings. I have constructed a table to help you with this.

It will be very hard for you to complete this immediately as you are unlikely to know the exact numbers, so take your time filling it out. I don't want you to guess in this section as it is incredibly important that you know the exact figures that are coming in and going out each month. Look over each row and decide how much you are spending in each category. This is much easier to do with your fixed expenses than your variable ones, but write down what you think it is going to be anyway. Before you begin, it might be a good exercise to review your bank statements, receipts or invoices which will help you complete the table as accurately as possible.

INCOME	Budget	Actual	Difference
Wages and Tips			
Interest Income			
Dividends			
Gifts Received			
Refunds/Reimbursements			
Transfer from Savings			
Other			
Other			
Total INCOME			

HOME EXPENSES	Budget	Actual	Difference
Mortgage/Rent			
Home/Rental Insurance			
Electricity			
Gas/Oil			
Water/Sewer/Trash			
Phone			
Cable/Satellite			
Internet			

Furnishings/Appliances			
Lawn/Garden			
Maintenance/Supplies			
Improvements			
Other			
Total **HOME EXPENSES**			
TRANSPORTATION	**Budget**	**Actual**	**Difference**
Vehicle Payments			
Auto Insurance			
Fuel			
Bus/Taxi/Train Fare			
Repairs			
Registration/License			
Other			
Total TRANSPORTATION			
HEALTH	**Budget**	**Actual**	**Difference**
Health Insurance			
Doctor/Dentist			
Medicine/Drugs			
Health Club Fees			
Life Insurance			
Veterinarian/Pet Care			
Other			
Total HEALTH			
CHARITY/GIFTS	**Budget**	**Actual**	**Difference**
Gifts Given			
Charitable Donations			
Religious Donations			
Other			
Total CHARITY/GIFTS			

SUBSCRIPTIONS	Budget	Actual	Difference
Newspaper			
Magazines			
Dues/Memberships			
Other			
Total SUBSCRIPTIONS			

DAILY LIVING	Budget	Actual	Difference
Groceries			
Personal Supplies			
Childcare			
Clothing			
Education/Lessons			
Dining/Eating Out			
Salon/Barber			
Pet Food			
Other			
Total DAILY LIVING			

ENTERTAINMENT	Budget	Actual	Difference
Videos/DVDs			
Music			
Games			
Rentals			
Movies/Theatre			
Concerts/Plays			
Books			
Hobbies			
Film/Photos			
Sports			
Outdoor Recreation			
Toys/Gadgets			
Vacation/Travel			
Other			
Total ENTERTAINMENT			

SAVINGS	Budget	Actual	Difference
Emergency Fund			
Transfer to Savings			
Retirement			
Investments			
Education			
Other			
Total SAVINGS			

OBLIGATIONS	Budget	Actual	Difference
Student Loan			
Other Loan			
Credit Cards			
Alimony/Child Support			
Property Tax			
Miscellaneous Tax			
Other			
Total OBLIGATIONS			

MISCELLANEOUS	Budget	Actual	Difference
Bank Fees			
Postage			
Other			
Other			
Total MISCELLANEOUS			

MONTHLY BUDGET SUMMARY	Budget	Actual	Difference
Total Income			
Total Expenses			
NET			

I imagine that 90 percent of the people I ask to carry out this exercise will say it was a pain to complete. But I'm certain that 100 percent of those people would also agree that they were amazed by the results.

I ask people to look over each row and give it some thought. What numbers leap out at you? Is the amount you are spending on a particular category appropriate? Are you spending what is considered to be normal on an item? For example, if you are paying €200 each month for life assurance, are you paying too much? Or if, for example, you are spending €300 on meals or takeaways every month, is that too much?

I was working with a client of mine recently who was having cash flow problems. At the end of each month she was back in her overdraft and was spending about €500 extra each month than she was earning, so she had a problem. She could not understand this because she did not go out much and she did not have much of a social life, so where was she going wrong? The first thing we did was complete the table.

She completed it and as she finished, she said that numbers just started to jump off the page at her, for example, she had a cleaning lady come to her house once a week, which was costing her €50 every time. This was adding up to over €2,500 per year. She knew it was costing her that much in her head but until she wrote it down, she did not realise that it was completely unnecessary. Due to her work commitments away from home, she felt that she needed a cleaner to maintain the house. But did she need a cleaner once a week? Of course she didn't, so she cut back to having the cleaner in every fortnight, which was going to save her €100 each month.

She also looked at how much she was spending at the off-license and on takeaway food as well. It was costing her about €600 each month and again the reason for this was she would get home late and the idea of having to cook a meal at 8PM was not appealing, so it was easier to get a takeout. So, rather than stopping altogether, she just cut back to spending €500 each month rather than €600, saving herself another €100 each month.

In just ten minutes she was able to find €200 each month that could now be redirected to a savings account or reallocated as she liked, but the point was, without analysing what she was spending her money on each month, she would never have discovered these two areas.

When I give presentations to companies on this subject, my advice is always the same: spend as much as you can on the things you like but don't spend money on the things you don't. Certainly spend €100 each month on your gym membership if you like going to the gym and it gives you pleasure. Spend €100 each month for your sports' subscription if you love sports. Don't spend money on golf membership if you play once or twice each year (and I put my hands up here – this was me! I paid €800 every year for golf membership but only played once or twice a year. I kept telling myself that I should stay a member because there would come a time when I would use it more. But I was merely trying to convince myself to justify the annual subscription until I got sense). Don't spend money on things you don't use and even if the cost each month is very small, don't continue paying it.

You spend the majority of your waking hours trying to earn a living. Don't you think you should make sure that this time is worth it? That is exactly the point of examining where your money goes each month.

I want you to look again at your outgoings and examine them to see if there are any expenses that can be eliminated altogether. For example, can you sell one of your cars? Is this possible or even feasible? If it is, would you have only one car loan instead of two? Can you trade down your car to a cheaper one and have a lower monthly repayment? If you stop using your credit cards and work hard to clear them off in full, suddenly you will have no more monthly credit card payments.

Look at what you spend on eating out, snacks, coffees, lunches, clothing, subscriptions, life assurance premiums, home insurance premiums, and seriously consider how you can reduce these or any other costs. For example, you might bring your lunch to work one week per month where you could save about €50. I will give you lots of money savings tips shortly.

If you want to improve your finances or you want to get out of debt, then you have to track your spending, because ultimately, the truth, although it will annoy the heck out of you at times, will set you free. The key to following a budget is to use a spending plan, and once you have one in place, everything else will fall in line. It will only take a few minutes to set up and record each week but it will give you a good idea of your spending and saving habits, as well as where you may need to make some changes.

It is all about recording your financial habits and then being willing to change those habits based on the results you get. I keep telling people that a spending plan is one of the most powerful tools available to help you free up extra money and improve your financial life. It allows you to have control over your money rather than it controlling you.

The 60 Percent Solution

Another question that I am frequently asked is just how much money I should be saving and spending on a monthly basis. The optimum amount you should be saving each month is 10 percent of your net, after-tax salary. For some people this is just not achievable but again, just because you can't start at 10 percent doesn't mean that you shouldn't start at all. Start at 1 percent of your salary and gradually increase that over time.

The editor-in-chief of MSN Money, Richard Jenkins, wrote an article some time ago called the '60% Solution' in which he suggests that you should spend your money the following way:

- 60 percent on food, utilities, mortgages, insurance, fuel etc.
- 10 percent on retirement savings
- 10 percent on long-term savings
- 10 percent on short-term savings for those irregular expenses that appear from time to time
- 10 percent on 'fun money'

Admittedly these figures were aimed at a younger generation but this idea, and there are many others like it, put forward the theory that you should break down your income into different sections and try live off 60 percent of it whilst saving and spending the other 40 percent.

How about starting off with spending 97 percent of your net monthly income on mortgages, utilities, transport etc. and save 1 percent into your emergency fund account and 1 percent into your savings account and the remaining 1 percent used to overpay on your debts each month? Why not start off like this and then in year two, if you can, your split might be 94 percent on essentials, with 2 percent in your emergency fund, 2 percent in your savings account and 2 percent towards your debts?

Do a risk test

After you have recorded what comes in and out of your account each month, are you left with a surplus? Are you spending way more than you are earning or are you breaking even? As I have alluded to already, there is no hiding from the numbers; you need to record them to find out how you are doing. You do not have to work for NASA to figure out where you are at.

So, let's dig a little bit deeper and find out how bad or good your situation is. What I want you to do first is add up your seven critical expenses, payments that have to be paid no matter what happens. What are they? Look at your worksheet, and add up the seven expenses that you could not go without paying; they may include some of the following:

- Mortgage/rent payments
- Food
- Utilities
- Fuel/transportation
- Children's expenses
- Gas/oil
- Phone
- Medicines
- Child support
- Life/health insurance premium

Now add up your seven critical expenses and divide them into your net monthly income to see what percentage goes to cover these outgoings. It could look something like this:

Income/Expenses	
Net Monthly Income	€3,500
My Seven Critical Expenses	€1,700
Result	49%

In this case, 49 percent of your net take-home pay accounts for the seven critical expenses each month, which is very high. Obviously mortgage repayments will make up a large part of most people's outgoings and is a must-spend, but the amount you need to get to for this exercise is less than 40 percent, so what can be realistically done to reduce this amount?

After you have completed this exercise, I want you to ask yourself the following:

- If I lost my job today, how many months would I be able to keep paying my bills?

- If my car broke down, or I needed to repair some part of my home that was damaged, how would I pay for that?

- If my partner lost their job or fell ill, how would I cover their expenses?

- If the tenants in our investment property moved out, how long could we make the mortgage repayments?

Your financial first aid kit

If the potential consequences of any of these things happening are bad, then more than anything else you need to establish what is commonly known as an emergency fund. This is typically six months' worth of your net income in a savings account, so that if anything unexpected happens, you have funds available.

When it comes to your emergency fund, you should try to accumulate this amount before you start attacking your debt.

This is very important, so please take note. Try and get your emergency fund accumulated as fast as possible and this can be done by tackling those seven critical expenses just discussed, rather than simply multiplying your salary by six. It would take you years to accumulate this amount and with such an overwhelming challenge facing you, you might not even start.

So, what are the top seven things that have to be paid if you needed to use your emergency fund? Look over your income and outgoings again. What are the must-pay items on your list? Let me help you a little bit, they might be something like these:

Rent/Mortgage	€
Fuel	€
Groceries	€
Insurance	€
Loan	€
Utilities	€
Oil/Heating	€
Total Seven Expenses	€
Amount needed to cover six months' expenses	€

Even if you are working off a deficit each month or you are on a low income, it may seem hard to set aside money for an emergency fund, but you really have to: don't underestimate the need for such a fund. Without any rainy day money to fall back on, you risk falling into debt every time a domestic crisis strikes – whether a car breaks down, a washing machine packs in etc.

So, it is worth trying to build up at least some emergency savings. Starting small and gradually building this amount up is the way forward, rather than saving nothing at all because you think it's too small to make a difference.

What about having your savings debited 'at source' directly from your salary each week or month so you don't even have it to see it in the first place? Ask your employer if this is possible.

What is your percent?

Here is another good exercise I want you to to do: figure out the amount of your monthly debt repayments as a percentage of your net monthly income.

Let me show you another example of this in operation. Let's assume a single person or a couple have a total net monthly income of €4,000 and they have credit card payments, mortgage/rent, car loan, personal loan payments that add up to €1,750 per month:

Monthly Debt as a Percentage of Monthly Income	
Net Monthly Income	€4,000
Minimum Monthly Loan Repayments	€1,750
Result	44%

In this case 44 percent of their net monthly income is going towards servicing their debt repayments each month. Ideally, you need to be aiming for no more than 25 percent each month in this area, so find out what your percentage is and start doing something about it.

Here is another exercise that will shock you. If you examined the breakdown of that €1,750 in my last example and looked at the amount of interest being paid within that €1,750, it could be as much as €750, meaning that the amount of interest being paid is 18 percent – nearly a fifth of your monthly income! Does that not make you want to tear your hair out? This was what the table looks like:

Monthly Interest on Debt as a Percentage of Monthly Income	
Net Monthly Income	€4,000
Monthly Payments Made Up Of Interest	€750
Result	18%

It always amazes me that if a bank is willing to lend you an amount up to 40 percent, for example, of your net monthly income, people will borrow the full amount available to them. A bank is not doing this out of goodness or generosity, they are simply using criteria to evaluate whether you are good for the money or not, which in turn will lead to profits for them – not you.

Unfortunately, in the recent past people borrowed as much as a bank was willing to lend and are now in a difficult financial situation. I am not here to pass judgement; what I am trying to show you is that by carrying out these exercises, you can clearly evaluate your situation, try do something about it and not make the same mistakes again in the future. If you allow a bank, merchandiser or credit card company to dictate how much you should spend and borrow, and you fall for their advice, you will end up paying them for the rest of your life – just ask anyone who is now paying a 100 percent mortgage for the next forty years.

Have you ever heard of the Parkinson Law? Although unknown to most of us, this law is one of the most important laws of money. First developed by an Englishman called C. Northcote Parkinson, the law states that expenses rise to meet income. It is a very simple theory but it explains why most people struggle financially all of their lives and don't achieve any of their financial goals. The law states that no matter how much money people earn, they tend to spend that exact amount and a little bit more besides. Their expenses rise in line with what they earn. Many people even today are earning much more than they did ten years ago, but they seem to need every single cent to maintain their current standard of living. No matter how much they make, there never seems to be enough.

The Parkinson Law states that only when you develop sufficient willpower to spend less than you earn will you start to improve your finances. The key here is to spend less than your income and, by saving and investing the difference, you can become financially free in your lifetime.

I met a client recently who was earning €6,500 per month and her outgoings were €4,500. She had a surplus of €2,000 each month. What she decided to do, consciously or unconsciously, was to borrow more money by moving to a new house (she had no reason to do this as she loved her existing one) because her bank was willing to lend her the money and she was able to afford the new higher monthly repayment. Because she earned €6,500 each month, she was in a rush to spend €6,500 each month – the Parkinson Law in action.

Of course only after having to take a 20 percent reduction in her salary does she start to regret ever having borrowed that money from her bank in the first place.

The same applies to credit cards. Why are we always in a rush to spend what the credit card company says we can? One reason could simply be down to the way information is phrased on their monthly statements, cleverly emphasising the amount we have 'available to spend'. Would it change our way of thinking if our monthly statement instead highlighted the amount we have 'available to borrow', and the fact that at 18 percent, if we pay the minimum payment each month it will take us twenty years to repay the debt in full? I think it might.

Finding out what percent of your salary is going toward debt payments is a very uncomfortable exercise – I know, I did it myself many years ago. However, it provided me with the motivation I needed to turn things around. When I looked at the amount I was paying back to lenders I got so angry at myself that I immediately decided enough was enough and that I was not going to work fifteen days out of thirty each month just to pay back my bank.

I resolved to become financially beholden to no one and by taking account of where I was and where I wanted to be, my motivation was further strengthened. I began my 'war' on my creditors by drawing up a plan of action. General Norman Schwarzkopf once said, 'Once the outcome has been determined, every other consideration and evaluation has to be made with this outcome in mind.' That is exactly how I felt.

Liam's Action List

- Prepare your net worth statement – draw a line down the middle of an A4 page. On the left-hand side, write down everything you own and what you think the value of it is. On the right-hand side, write down everything you owe. Subtract one from the other and this will give you your current net worth.

- Know what you are up against. List every single debt you owe. Record this by doing what I showed you earlier in this chapter: starting with who you owe this money to, the amount outstanding, the monthly repayment, the term remaining and the interest rate charged.

- Complete an income and expenditure form for a typical month. Record how much comes in each month and how much goes out. Put a figure alongside the categories I provided for you. Add up all the numbers and see whether you have a surplus or a deficit each month.

- Add up your top seven most important expenses and that is the figure you need to save and have in your emergency fund. This is your first financial goal above any other and until you have this amount in place, you will find it difficult to move on to other goals like getting out of debt as fast as you can. Start off with an amount you can afford, even if it is just 1percent of your monthly net income.

'Never spend your money before you have it.'

–**Thomas Jefferson**

05

What is a Budget?

This is a question I am often asked and the very mention of the word conjures up images of Ebenezer Scrooge, and is immediately considered something time-consuming, boring and unpleasant. However, this couldn't be further from the truth and it is crucial that you start thinking differently about budgets, otherwise all of your efforts will come to nothing.

A budget is a plan, that's about the best description I can give it. It's a plan for where you want your money to go each month; it's a breakdown of how much you make and how much you spend.

People who don't have a budget, and maybe you are one of them, don't get into debt because of a lack of money, they go into debt because they spend more than they make. They don't have a plan.

Using a budget will help you to develop good spending habits by preventing you from spending more than you earn. It ensures that you have money available to cover your expenses and that you set aside money each month that can be used in the event of an emergency, for example.

A budget gets you focused on what is really important to you and allows you to value your time and effort at work much more. Let me explain what I mean by this: let's say you work a forty-hour week, your hourly pay therefore is about half your annual salary. So, let's assume your salary is €30,000 per year; halve this and divide by 1,000, this means that your hourly rate of pay is about €15.

The next time you are tempted to spend €90 on something on a whim, ask yourself, 'Is this worth six hours of my working day?' I am going to have to work from 9AM to 3PM next Monday to pay for these shoes that I don't really need. It makes you stop and think, particularly for those impulse purchases. I don't want you to think this way all of the time or feel guilty when you do indulge from time to time; you should, you deserve to, but for those things that you don't really need, maybe think twice and start valuing your time a bit more, it will drastically improve your finances.

Here's one final thought: if you could reduce your outgoings by €100, have you ever considered what that money would be worth if you saved it each month instead of spending it? If you deposited it in an account that returned 8 percent each year, after five years you would have more than €7,000.

Just give it some thought; the more you spend, the less you have to save. So every time you are spending money needlessly on things you don't need, you are prolonging your ability to become mortgage-free, fund your children's education or retire early.

I am going to finish this section by giving you some more ideas on how you should start to approach your budget each month. If you begin to follow what I suggest, you will see budgeting in a whole new light – let me reiterate again that devising and following your budget each month will lead you to make better financial decisions and will dramatically improve your finances.

- The budget doesn't control you, you control it.

- By having a budget in place that you track and follow, *you* decide what your priorities are and *you* decide where your hard-earned money goes. Identifying what you spend your money on each month will help you fund the really important things in your life. For example, did you know that the cost of one less cappuccino per day would reduce the term of a €300,000 mortgage from thirty years to twenty-eight years! Who would have thought that the cost of one coffee per day, if applied as an overpayment on your mortgage, could take two years off the term? And you will notice I didn't say give up drinking cappuccinos, I said one less. So, what is that thing that, you can cut back on? What is that one item that you could do without that if used somewhere else, could make a significant impact on your financial well-being? A written budget will help you identify what it is.

- A budget is about awareness, it's not about cutting back or denying yourself.

- A budget gives you the ability to save more money, and for some people it shows that they should be spending more money in certain areas, but it isn't about squeezing the enjoyment out of your life. It simply allows you to get much more for your money than you have up to this point, and it focuses you on getting the best value for your money and helps you to spend with the long term in mind.

- There is no single budget that works for everyone, what works for you is the best budget.

Once you have begun to monitor your budget, it is crucial not to abandon the idea after a month or two because it's not working the way you want it to, or it is proving a chore to go over your bank statements and check receipts to see what you have spent your money on. If you monitor your spending on a daily basis and just record how much you spent and on what in a journal, notebook or better still on a document saved on your computer, you will easily stay on top of your income and outgoings.

Keep your budget current

Your monthly budget should be an ongoing process. Just as you are supposed to look at your bills and statements each month, sit down and examine your budget. This will keep you completely up to date with your finances and, in addition to keeping your knowledge current, you will be able to see what progress you are making.

I have put together a spending plan template on page 70 for a typical month, which I want you to use and record on a monthly basis. Apportion an amount each month to a particular category and make sure that you track what you are spending each month, knowing that you have a certain amount that you have budgeted for and cannot exceed.

Finally, if you find that you are consistently off in a particular category, perhaps you need to re-evaluate the budget. A budget isn't set in stone – you can adjust it if it's not working for you. The important thing is to start planning and know where your money goes. If you don't have a plan for your money, it will disappear on meaningless items. By making a plan and sticking to it, you can ensure that you are doing what you can to achieve your financial goals. Without a plan, your goals are just dreams. Also, the best plan in the world is useless if we don't act on it!

A Canadian study found that people who stuck to a budget had a higher net worth than those who didn't or had one they didn't follow, so get budgeting!

The power of cash envelopes

Despite the help of useful computer software or fancy notebooks, some people find it extremely difficult to monitor and track their monthly finances. What can be done for people who just can't budget?

The answer lies in using cash only for spending purposes, and to assist in this, I often ask people to work out of 'cash envelopes' for specific categories, for example groceries, entertainment, clothing and food.

What I suggest to these people is that every month, *before* their money comes in, they should sit down and work out what they are going to spend their money on for the next month.

By doing this simple exercise, you force your money to behave, and at the end of the month, your income versus outgoings should equal zero. This usually takes about twenty minutes to do each month.

How do you decide how much to put into each envelope? This is worked out through trial and error in the beginning, as you learn which categories you are likely to spend on impulse. These categories are where you are most likely to overspend if you use the debit card.

Here are some of the categories that people use cash envelopes for:

- Groceries
- Dining out
- Clothing
- Entertainment
- Money to blow

Think about these categories for a moment – it's easy to overspend on each one. But by using cash envelopes, you know for sure that you will not overspend. You will only spend the amount you budget for. If you set aside €50 this month for takeaways and the last week of the month arrives and you go to your envelope marked 'Takeout' and there is nothing in it, then sorry, no takeaway until next week.

If you were using a debit card, I can guarantee that you would overspend each month. Why?

Your debit card doesn't allow you to keep a running amount of how much you have left to spend for each category, whereas with cash envelopes, you can just open it and count! Hey presto, you immediately know how much you have left for the month.

I normally only suggest this course of action for people who struggle to manage their finances, and it might be worth considering for a month or two. This exercise really just gets people into the habit of watching what they spend each month and prevents them from overspending.

If you ask anyone who does this or has done it in the past, they will all tell you it works. It is fool-proof.

Finally, I was reading about a couple recently who were both in their eighties and had been married for over sixty years. They told a story that, back in the fifties and sixties, banks were an absolute no-go for ordinary people – you could not even open a bank account unless you had a large amount to give them. So what did they do with their weekly wages? They kept them in a shoe box! And to help them budget, the box was split into different sections, such as food, clothes, electricity and so on. They went on to explain that although money was tight, they didn't run into debt because if they could not afford it, they simply didn't buy it. This resulted in them always being careful with money as it became more freely available. Being prudent and valuing money was ingrained in them from an early age. Their take on people's money worries now is that people relied too much on banks for money, use cards to pay for things and then lose track of what they are spending. Wise words indeed.

Liam's Action List

- Review the individual budget categories where you spend the most money. If you can trim 5 or 10 percent from these categories it can make a big difference each month.

- Plan your spending before the month begins so you know what you are going to spend your money on in advance rather than wondering at the end of the month where it all went.

- Identify three areas in your outgoings each month that you want to cut back on. If you spend €100 on clothes or takeaways, resolve to spend just €80 in this category for the following month. Deposit the €20 saving into your savings account at the start of the month, not at the end. You have to see the benefit of cutting back, so save the amount in a separate savings account that you can't get easy access to.

- Use cash whenever possible. Take out enough cash to last one week at a time. Make up your mind that the cash you have is all you get for discretionary spending each week. It's much easier to turn down a €60 pair of shoes when it will take the last of your week's cash than it is when you just have to swipe a credit card.

- At the end of each day, record what you spent money on and how much. The results will give you a great idea of what your spending and saving habits are, but more importantly it will help you see where you may need to make some changes.

- Share the responsibility. Make sure you're not the only member of your household concerned about your budget. Sit down together and determine how much spending money you should each have. Then, check in every week to see how well you're doing. If the entire family shares the responsibility for the budget, everyone can cut back just a little and make a big difference. One person shouldn't have to shoulder the entire burden alone.

- If you feel that your budget is off target, then amend it for the following month. It will be hard to get it exactly right straight away, it will take at least two or three months before you can get an exact handle on where your money is going and whether you are setting aside too much or too little in each category.

- Be realistic, and don't set yourself a budget amount that is too small and that you simply can't keep to.

- Include once-off things that you will need money for like Christmas, birthdays and property tax in your monthly budget. Set aside an amount you will need for these once-off payments even if it's twelve months away. By doing this, that large once-off payment won't hurt your income so much when the time arrives.

- Budget for impulses. We are all human and yes we do need to spend money on ourselves because it may make us feel a little bit better and sometimes we simply deserve to as well.

'It is flagrantly dishonest for an advertising agent to urge consumers to buy a product which he would not allow his own wife to buy.'

—David Ogilvy

06

Tackling Consumerism

There is a phenomenon that has affected us all at some stage in our lives; it is called consumerism. It is associated with happiness when you buy something. Have you ever referred to someone (or maybe you have been referred to) as a 'shopaholic' or have you ever heard the term 'retail therapy?' Both terms jokingly describe someone who shops for fun or has a need to buy items when they shop. They do not need the item, they simply want it and enjoy the act of buying new things. Not everyone suffers from this condition but many people do and get into debt as a consequence.

Many organisations take advantage of our vulnerability and they invest billions each year to create, grow and maximise their ability to get us off the sofa, on the phone or down to their stores to make a purchase.

When you go to your local supermarket to do your weekly shopping, do you think they just randomly select what aisles to put what in? Of course not. They spend millions of euros in order to research the most effective ways in which to encourage and seduce us into buying and spending more than we need – sweets and magazines placed by the till, store layouts make us walk the whole distance, eye-level products etc.

What about the buy-one-get-one-free approach, or the get-the-second-one-half-price deals? How many times have we been suckered into purchasing them? What about the '50 percent off' sign we see that entices us to purchase because we think we are getting a great deal? Unfortunately, they are not always the great money-savers they seem to be. All of these 'bargains' are designed to exploit our impulses and can be either great or terrible. Put simply, they are good if the item you purchase won't go off and you would buy it anyway – toothpaste, batteries etc. But it's good to remember that if you didn't buy the '50 percent off' deal at all, you would be guaranteed 100 percent off! So, the next time you see these discounts think of them as if it's 50 percent on. And remember: don't buy them if you think you are not going to use them!

Supermarkets have a ploy and they want us to buy more than we need – research proves this. Across the Irish Sea, in the UK consumers waste 4.4 million tonnes of food each year. They throw away 32 percent of the bread they buy, 24 percent of their vegetables, 20 percent of their fruit and 17 percent of their cereals. When you think of the amount of money that is wasted, it is huge. Do you think here in Ireland that we are the same? You can bet your house on it.

The marketing strategies that supermarkets and the like employ are actually brilliantly simple. They are so effective because they know what influences us at the deepest level so that we end up wanting something so badly that we will do anything to get it. Think about this for a second. They get us to spend money, money we may not even have, and pay a high price for it, all because of our desire to feed the need, the need for instant gratification that they helped create in the first place. And you know, most of the things that we end up buying we didn't need at all, we just needed to buy it!

So, how do we get suckered into buying things we don't need? Well one of the most powerful tools exploited by retailers is creating the illusion that all things are affordable. They do this by breaking the overall cost into many small payments over a period of time.

Many items we would really like right now may be beyond our purchasing power because we don't have the cash to buy them, but if we spread the payments out over a couple of years, there should be no problem. Why wait to save when you can get it right now? That 50-inch plasma TV that costs €2,500 now only costs €42 per month over five years. Happy days, I'll sign up for that.

A good friend of mine was telling me a story about how he and his wife had nothing to do one Sunday so they decided to go for a walk around a shopping centre. They went there with no intention of buying anything, they just wanted to kill a few hours and spend some time together browsing the shops. They went into a furniture shop and saw a bed advertised for sale at €1,000, down from €1,200 and the great thing was that they could finance this at 0 percent over twelve months. They didn't need a bed, the one they had was perfectly fine, but this was a great-looking new bed and their minds start playing tricks on them. They started to find fault in their own two-year-old bed and decided they couldn't pass up such a great offer. So, they signed on the dotted line, agreed to a finance deal over twelve months without looking at the terms and conditions and later that night they were sleeping in their new bed.

A couple of months later my friend's wages were late arriving in his account by a day or two and the direct debit to pay the bed was missed. He duly received a letter from the company that financed his bed purchase stating that a payment was missed and under the terms and conditions of the agreement they both signed the 0 percent offer was now withdrawn and replaced by an interest rate of . . . wait for it . . . 27 percent. The bed that they didn't need and one they had bought for €1,000 ended up costing them €1,270, more than the full price of the bed was before it was reduced!

Some retailers are predators and they exploit our incredible desire for instant gratification. Why do we have to wait and save for two years to have something when we can have it now, or simply put the cost of it on our credit card? We have got to recognise what these retailers are trying to do and stop falling for their gimmicks.

However, I recognise that this is not easy. I was astonished while researching this topic to find that as consumers, we are exposed to an average of 5,000 brand messages per day. Isn't that just incredible? It is also remarkable that according to research carried out recently, a housewife under the age of fifty is exposed to between eighteen and twenty-five minutes of television advertising each day in most countries. Every evening, during prime-time shows, a viewer is exposed to between 100 and 150 commercials! Again, these figures amazed me as they applied only to television; what about the attempts to get our attention via radio, the internet, cinema, advertisement billboards, newspapers and so on? That is not to mention the TV channels dedicated purely to shopping – you don't even have to get off the sofa, all you need is a credit card and a phone.

You might be saying, yeah so what, I might watch the adverts in between *Coronation Street* but that's all I do – watch them. However, and this has been scientifically proven, without any special effort on our part, our brain records the information we see and hear subconsciously. Our brains, whether you know it or not, chooses what interests us and stores this information in our brains at a subconscious level so that we will at some stage in the future act upon it. Banks did the same thing. They sent us letters saying we were pre-approved for loans and whilst we didn't immediately act upon what they were offering us, we stored the approval in our brains and at some stage found a reason to use the loan they were offering.

I am going to let you in on a secret that only those in the marketing industry know and being aware of this, I assure you will improve your finances no end. Marketers know you store information from their adverts in your subconscious that you may not immediately act upon. They deliberately present the advert or message to us as often as possible so that when your guard eventually does lower, you will act and buy their product. That's what marketing companies keep telling their clients; you will become successful only by repetition. There is no point in advertising your product for ten days each year and being silent the rest of the year. You have to 'whisper in the consumer's ear' all year round.

So, let them whisper all they like, just let it in one ear and out the other.

Another reason we buy things has got nothing to do with TV or radio adverts, but is instead initiated and propagated entirely by ourselves. People buy things or upgrade from what they already have, so that they can be the envy of their family, friends and neighbours. Yes, they may be attracted to new features on the latest phone or they really like the look and feel of a new model of car, but the reason they are buying is to either keep up, or be better than, the Joneses.

Let me tell you one thing, which some of you may find hard to believe but it is almost certainly true – the Joneses are in debt as well. Unless you know for an absolute fact that your neighbours have millions in cash sitting in their bank account, don't assume you know their financial position, know only your own.

There are two women I know that are clients of mine and one drives a one-year-old, state-of-the-art people carrier, which was bought for about €65,000. She drives to my office looking for financial advice in this car and your first impressions are: what a car! This person must be doing great for themselves and earning lots of money. My second client drives to my office in an eight-year-old car. One wheel guard is missing but otherwise it looks a fine car.

So, who do you think is the wealthiest? Obviously, from how they dress and what they drive, you would think the person driving the new car is much wealthier. However, this person drives to me looking for advice on how to deal with her creditors because she is so in debt it's scary. Her beautiful car has not been taxed in about three months because she can't afford it. She is a month behind with her car repayments but again, outwardly she is showing all the trappings of doing very well for herself and money does not appear to be an issue for her.

My client with the eight-year-old car drives to me looking for different advice and has different problems. Her problem is that she has no car loan or any other loan for that matter and has been saving for the last number of years, so her problem is what she should do with the €100,000 she has saved over the past twelve years. Where should she put the money, what account is offering the best rate of return? She may not look very wealthy but she doesn't have that need to impress people. She doesn't worry about what people think of her driving an older car because (a) she doesn't care and (b) nobody is, in fact, saying anything about her car. People have enough to worry about themselves than how old your car is.

Please do not be influenced by what car your friend, brother, sister, neighbour or work colleague drives, or what they wear, how many holidays they go on each year or how many 'investment properties' they have. Make your lifestyle and purchasing decisions based on what you can afford and not what your friends are buying.

A word to the wise: the women I was talking about who looked very wealthy but in fact was in serious financial difficulty wanted a solution from me that did not involve her trading down from her big car or giving up her two holidays a year, etc. Our conversation did not go very well because I was honest with her; if she wanted to beat the debt problems that were getting between her and her night's sleep, she would have to lay everything on the table and be willing to make changes and sacrifices. I told her it was better to lose this particular battle in order to win her war on debt in the long run. It was better to sell her car and not go on those holidays right now and plan to buy another nice car in the future when her finances would allow her to, than it is to see everything come crashing down around her and end up losing everything.

It is important to see the bigger picture with regard to these things. I love the fact, for example, that I don't pay anyone anything for my car and instead of feeling envious of people driving a bigger or newer car than me, I mostly feel slightly sorry for them because I know how much they must be paying each month and smug in another way because of the amount I am saving each month into my retirement account. I guess it is all about feeling secure and confident with yourself and valuing what you want to achieve in the long term.

Let me give you a couple of tips before you make those big purchases in the future:

- Do I really need this item?
- Am I buying it because I need it or because of what people will think of me for having it?

If you consider both questions before you make that next big purchase, and you are honest with your answer, then I am sure you won't fall victim to consumerism or what you imagine others will think of you and your finances will improve dramatically. The basic idea here is to change the way you think about spending. This is not going to happen overnight, because the way we have been programmed to spend our money has been formed over a number of years and it will take time to alter our habits.

Liam's Action List

- Don't get suckered in by buy-now-pay-later offers. It's just retailers getting you to spend money that you don't have on things that you don't need.

- Save before you buy. Although that's not always possible, particularly for bigger purchases, you can still save money that can go a long way towards the cost of the item you are considering buying. This will reduce the amount you may have to borrow in the future and lower your monthly repayment.

- Don't buy things just because your neighbours or friends have them. 'The Joneses' are in debt too, so why buy things and get into debt just to keep up appearances?

- Before you decide to purchase something, sleep on it and then decide whether it is something you still want twenty-four hours later. If it is something that you still really need then buy it, if it is something that you really want, then by all means buy it, but buy it with cash, and not on credit.

- If you are going to buy something and you don't have the cash, then investigate before you borrow. Look at borrowing as 'buying money'. Comparison shop to find the best bargain available, whether you're shopping for money through a bank, a finance company, or applying for a new credit card.

- Beware of the large print! Nothing down, no interest or low interest may look attractive but such offers are frequently filled with fees and penalties that can turn ugly if you get in a pinch. Always read the fine print!

- Spend with the long term in mind. Financially successful people see a euro not for what it is worth to them at the moment, but what it will be worth to them in the future, and you should do the same thing.

'My problem lies in reconciling my gross habits with my net income.'
—**Errol Flynn**

07

It All Adds Up!

Sometimes when I meet people and they begin analysing their income and outgoings and find areas that they can cut back on, they become a little bit disheartened when the amount they can find is only, say, €5 per day. However, €5 might not seem much in the course of one day, but if you think of what €5 would become over the course of one year, it is significant.

So, when you are looking at cost-saving exercises, think of them in terms of one year, not one day. For example, if you save €5 each day, you are going to have €1,825 in twelve months' time, not bad hey? If you saved this amount over twenty years, guess how much you would have in your account . . . ? €114,854!

Reducing your spending on non-essential items and saving the difference is one of the best ways to create savings and eliminate debt and monitoring what you spend your money on each day/week is the best way to find this extra money.

Now, don't get me started on cigarettes! As well as it being incredibly good for your health not to smoke, it is also very good for your finances. In terms of life assurance alone, you are probably going to pay as much as four times more than a non-smoker does.

I carried out an exercise recently where I looked at what the additional cost really means to a smoker and I found that for a person who smokes ten cigarettes a day, the actual cost to them in extra life and health insurance premiums, along with more medical fees and so on, is that every cigarette is costing them €4.50. Expensive habit.

I was working with a couple recently who were having trouble repaying their mortgage and a couple of personal loans. When I was analysing their expenses, I noticed that he was spending €3,146 every year on cigarettes. That amount would have paid his mortgage for seven months of the year but he was spending it on cigarettes. Now giving them up is easier said than done, I absolutely appreciate that, and I am sure this man had tried many times before, but he has got to try harder. Even if he cut back a little bit he could save an awful lot and I was trying to put the cost of each cigarette into context for him when telling him that his habit is the equivalent of seven months of mortgage payments. Hopefully this thought will make every cigarette he has taste a little less nice than before.

I am now going to give you some ideas on how you can reduce those outgoings a little bit more.

Ideas on reducing your outgoings

In these tough economic times, earning more money at work may be difficult, you may even be out of work, so first let's look at ways that you can increase your income by reducing your outgoings.

Get rid of your car loan repayment

I spoke earlier in the book about what I did, and let me tell you it works. I, like many others, had a car loan and was making regular payments each month to my lender. But what if you didn't have that car loan anymore, that money could then be used to pay off other debt or save more. I read recently that the average cost of a car loan is just under €400 each month and this is the amount that people continue to pay from their early twenties right up to their late sixties. What if I told you that if you saved that amount in a basic savings account instead, you would have over €1.5 million in it by the time you retire!

It seems astonishing that we pay over €1.5 million for the cost of driving a car in our lifetime, *if* we financed each purchase. On the other hand, if we didn't have that car loan we would end up being a millionaire. This is a fact, not a hypothetical scenario; if we didn't finance each car purchase over our lifetime, we would end up millionaires, it's as simple as that.

But, I need a car and I can't do without one and I don't have the money to but one outright. I hear you. So, finance your first car, make it a small economical one with a modest monthly payment and save €200 each month. In two years you will have €4,800 and you can now trade up your car to a newer, maybe bigger one and you use your cash. If you wait three years to trade up, now you will have €7,200 in savings towards a newer car. Can you see that if you start out small and save the amount you would have been paying for a bigger car at the start, in a relatively short space of time you could end up buying a car for cash!

Look at ways of trying to get rid of your existing car loan as fast as possible. That might mean trading down if you can, or paying more each month on your existing loan so that it is paid faster.

Buy generic

When you buy a brand-named product, the cost of advertising the product is built into the shelf price. When you see great adverts promoting a particular brand, often the cost of making this advert is transferred to the consumer through hefty cost prices. You are financing the cost of the TV/radio or newspaper advert. This means that you are paying more than you need to and why would you do that? Oftentimes a generic product has the same quality as the brand one, but you are buying at a lower price.

In supermarkets there are usually three brand levels:

- Supermarket own brand
- Mainstream brand
- Premium brand

This system automatically allows supermarkets to justify huge variations in price.

When we decide to buy something it is often based upon brand and not experience. What I mean is that we think if we choose to pay a higher price then it will taste nicer.

For example, you might have a supermarket advertising one of its products as its 'finest' so you assume it is high quality, whilst another of its brands might be called 'value', which suggests the product is cheap and nasty. You feel the price difference is legitimate. Who decides this? The supermarket of course – its packaging and product placement are all designed to support this myth.

We also think that if we decide to pay a higher price then it will taste nicer! My advice? *Taste with your mouth not with your eyes!*

I am not saying there is no difference in produce and production quality but there is no uniform guide to quality – this is something we need to judge ourselves.

I am also not suggesting that you always buy the 'no frills' brand either, but I want people to try and downshift.

To try this, occasionally try something one brand level cheaper. Sometimes you will like it and other times you won't. You might not notice the difference in a can of baked beans or a loaf of bread. Next time you want pasta sauce for example, get one of your normal ones and one supermarket brand and try them out.

An exercise was done recently where a person was tracked shopping and their weekly shopping was mimicked choosing one brand level lower than what they were purchasing.

The person's trolley bill came to €130 and the other was €95. The trolley with a brand level lower was 25 percent cheaper.

The following week they lived off the lower brand trolley and to their surprise only noticed the difference for half of the goods. Where they didn't see the difference, they simply switched and now their weekly shopping became €105 each week – a reduction of €25 per week.

Remember downshifting is about trying not switching.

- Downshift cleaning products and cosmetics
- Downshift your supermarket

Time trips to bag bigger reductions!

There are bargains to be had each day in supermarkets, especially on items that are near their sell-by dates. Reduction times vary but research carried out recently showed the following:

Amount you may be able to save

8AM to 10AM	4PM to 5PM	7PM to 9PM
Up to 25%off	Up to 50% off	Up to 75% off

Save on your credit card

You can do this by switching to a 0 percent provider immediately. If you are paying, for example, 17.4 percent on your current card and you transfer to a 0 percent rate then you will save yourself €71 in interest repayments each month, assuming a balance of just €5,000.

Even if you didn't switch to a 0 percent provider, by simply reducing the interest rate charged on your card, you could save yourself a tonne of money. For example:

Decrease in interest rate by	€5,000 debt over 1 year
1%	Save €50
3%	Save €150
5%	Save €250
10%	Save €500
18%	Save €900

Let us talk briefly about credit card minimum repayments. People think, 'well I paid the amount they asked me for on time, aren't I a responsible card holder?' Yes, you certainly are from the credit card company's point of view. They love customers who pay the minimum amount each month. Why? Your balance outstanding carried forward into the next month accrues interest!

The minimum payment is normally a certain percentage on the outstanding debt, normally between 2 percent and 3 percent, with a minimum payment of €10. The danger of paying the minimum payment is that as your debt gets smaller so does your minimum repayment, so your money is effectively being sucked into a compound interest sinkhole.

Let me give you an example of this. If you were thirty-three years of age, had a debt of €5,000 and paid the minimum amount each month – guess what age you would be when your debt was cleared in full? sixty-five! In that time you would have paid over €7,000 in interest.

This is the problem with minimum repayments. People often complain that they seem to be getting nowhere and they are right.

Cut down on those takeaways

Stop getting takeaways so often. Yes it's convenient, yes you like the food but it is expensive if you are buying them twice or three times each week. Why not try giving yourself a 'takeaway night' once a week? Again this is simply cutting back. Prepare a menu each week and prepare your food in advance.

Cut down on cappuccinos/chocolate bars/soft drinks

Again I am saying cut down, not give up altogether. One less per day will go a long way towards improving your finances. OK, let's do the math. One less cappuccino at €3 per day means a saving of €15 per week or €780 per year! If you applied the cost of just one cappuccino per day to a savings plan, you could accumulate €30,000 in ten years and €114,000 in twenty years. I was telling a friend of mine this and her reply, which was more of a scream, was 'are you telling me my cappuccinos are costing me €114,000?!'

Look at your wardrobe

Do you routinely buy a new piece of clothing on payday because you deserve it?

Every two or three months is a good time to plan your clothing purchases for the coming months.

Look at your wardrobe and decide what you really need for the next few months, whether it's for work or play. Planning for these purchases and budgeting for them will help you buy what you really need and want rather than simply snapping up whatever's on sale. This way you will not overspend on clothing that you just don't need – check and see how many items of clothing in your wardrobe still have a tag on them.

Cancel your club membership that you don't use

If you are not going to the gym at least twice a week or, for example, not playing golf at least twenty times a year then cancel your membership immediately. How many times have we promised ourselves that we will use 'the club' and 'sure isn't it good to have it'? Instead you could try getting some fresh air and exercise with a walk, cycle or run.

Cancel your movie/sports channel

A basic TV package should cost about €25 per month. However, this can cost as much as €70, if you want more channels. But how often do you really watch the movies available, and don't they play the same films over and over? What is there to watch on the sports channel, apart from a soccer match on a Sunday? Speedway, cricket, darts, American football, squash?

Only carry cash

One of the easiest ways to limit the amount you spend each week is to only carry cash with you. If you don't have access to that laser or credit card, then you will not be able to spend any of the money that is in your account (current account), or is not in your account (visa card).

It doesn't matter how much you want those new pair of shoes, or that new golf club or the new 50-inch TV, if you don't have enough cash for it, you can't buy it. I don't know about you, but I always did find it easier to spend €100 using a card than when I have to hand over €100 in cash. Something about physically parting with cash makes it harder to spend. When you use a debit or visa card, even on small purchases, they surprise you when the statement arrives and you realise just how much you have, in fact, spent. Handing over cash really brings home to you how much money you are actually spending.

A study carried out in 2011 found that people paying with cash think more about costs than those who use credit. Card-users dwell more on the benefits and subsequently pay more than they need to.

Sleep

Here is another great tool to use if you want to cut back on your outgoings each month. There really are very few things that you need to purchase that can't be bought the following day, so if you are faced with that temptation of buying something you don't really need, do your wallet or purse a favour and sleep on it.

I like watches and have plenty of them. I was out one weekend with my wife and kids when I saw a really nice watch. It cost about €100, so it wasn't very expensive, and I was really tempted to buy it. I didn't need it, but still, it was really nice and a bargain at €100; I could have had it immediately.

I decided to sleep on it and twenty-four hours later, my desire for the watch had reduced somewhat. I looked at my other watches and found one I hadn't worn in ages and it was like getting a new watch so I wore that for a while and I quickly forgot about that new one I had seen. It's amazing what a good night's sleep can do for you.

Someone once told me a very simple fact that I have always remembered: tailors make clothes and cut suits to make them fit. If a customer has a 36-inch waist then they make trousers to fit a 36-inch waist. How about applying this principle to your finances? This might be easy to say but harder to implement, but it can be done. It may mean you have to:

- Buy clothes from charity shops for a while
- Drink and socialise less
- Trade down your car
- Trade down your home
- Eat less takeaways
- Stay away from places of temptation, such as shopping centres or the city centre
- Do not shop with your friends, because you may end up spending money with them
- Stop using your car as often as you are – look at car pooling
- Sell things you never use

These are just some ideas on areas where you may be able to cut back. There are other areas that you should consider and I am now going to give you my Top 50 money saving tips. These are tips that can and will save you money, and if you go through this list and find four or five areas that you can apply and use in your daily life, then great, because when you combine it with the other cost reducing areas I have just referred to, they will save you hundreds of euros each year.

50 Money Saving Tips

1. Don't pay unnecessary fees to your bank or credit card company. Late fees and referral charges can cost you hundreds each year. Pay by direct debit each month from an account that is only used to pay bills, nothing else.

2. Shop around for home and life assurance premiums. Use an internet provider or an independent broker. I carried out this exercise for a client recently and saved her €679 in about five minutes because she was paying €379 more than she needed to for her life cover and €300 more for her home insurance.

3. Take good care of your house and car. Preventative maintenance is a lot less expensive than repair costs.

4. Changing your mobile phone provider can save you money. Make sure you match your plan with your usage. Don't pay for services that you don't use.

5. Always make a list before you go shopping and don't shop on an empty stomach, you will end up spending more.

6. Plan meals for the week ahead. This will cut out trips for Take aways, so keep your freezer stocked with good, quick-fix meals. Buy bargain-priced, in-season produce.

7. Avoid buying items at eye level in the supermarket. This is where the most expensive items are placed.

8. Cut out your bad habits – cut down or try to eliminate your alcohol and cigarette consumption.

9. Limit the amount of coffees you have each day. Yes they may be really good, but too many can be an awful waste of money. Coffee only costs a few cents per cup when it's made at home or brought to work.

10. Invite friends over instead of going out.

11. Don't spend a fortune on entertaining your children or buying them toys every time you go shopping. They can be entertained very inexpensively; an adventure in the park or made-up games can be great fun. I loved playing marbles as a child and I was telling my kids, so one day I bought a packet of marbles for €1.50, brought them home and I showed the three of them the games I used to play. Well, the fun we had seeing who could throw the marble closest to the wall was incredible – and all for €1.50.

12. Keep your car well maintained. Make it part of your routine to have it checked twice a year, it will keep it going for a year or two more than you thought, saving you monthly car repayments that can now be used to pay down debt.

13. Get your house re-valued – lenders can offer better rates if your mortgage is less than 50 percent of its value.

14. Rent out a room. You can earn up to €10,000 per year under the rent a room scheme.

15. Take in foreign students during the summer.

16. Avoid mortgage payment protection; it's a money racket for the insurance company.

17. Buy a used car. The minute you buy a new car it loses value. Do you think a 0 percent finance deal is good on a new car when the value of it goes down 20 percent when you drive it off the forecourt? It is a fact that most millionaires drive a second-hand car.

18. Shop around and compare the price in each dealership when buying a car.

19. Negotiate and haggle. Insist on the lowest price possible, make an offer and stick to your guns.

20. Buy small, it costs less.

21. Increase your home security – discounts can be had on your home insurance policy for such things as smoke detectors, burglar alarms etc.

22. Seek out discounts if you are a pensioner, you could get up to 10 percent off your home insurance premium.

23. Don't over-insure your property – insure it for its re-instatement value and not its market value.

24. Cut your food bill by as much as 20 percent by shopping at different stores. Compare prices from one store to another.

25. Try and shop on your own. Your 'little helpers' can add quite a bit to your bill, as we all know.

26. Don't shop for food when you are tired. You will end up buying more sweets and food high in carbohydrates.

27. Shop in the morning time. You will get through the store much faster, spending less.

28. Take the farmers market approach; buy produce that is fresh, inexpensive and in season at your local market.

29. Use your coupons! You will be surprised by how much they can save you.

30. Check your store for the discount section displaying goods that are about to expire, such as meat and bread. Use them that night or freeze them.

31. Beware of the 'buy one, get one free' offers.

32. Check your receipts! No matter how careful you or the store staff may be, mistakes do happen.

33. Check your local newspaper for advertisements of lunch and dinner specials and early bird specials.

34. Limit eating out for lunch every day; it's very expensive.

35. Buy one less cappuccino, soft drink or chocolate bar each week.

36. If you are going to eat out, eat out during the week rather than at weekends.

37. Eat out early. Lots of restaurants offer specials if you eat before 6pm. It's great if you are going to the cinema or for parents who need to make an early night of it.

38. The mark up on alcoholic beverages in restaurants is massive. Check and see if you can bring your own wine or, instead of having a drink with dinner, have a glass of wine when you get home.

39. Skip dessert. If you're eating at a sit-down restaurant, dessert is often a rip-off. Pick up a carton of ice cream on the way home, and save a fortune.

40. Try for student nights at hair salons.

41. Use rechargeable batteries.

42. Take out a magazine subscription if you buy the same magazine each month – it's cheaper!

43. Check out the local buy and sell for gym equipment then kit out your garage or side room – it's better value than joining a gym.

44. Cancel any unused digital/satellite TV channels.

45. Give up smoking.

46. Use energy-saving light bulbs.

47. Try house swapping for an alternative holiday.

48. Don't leave the heating on with the windows open.

49. When you are hiring any equipment do it over bank holidays so you get an extra free day's hire.

50. Use your library for internet access and books.

Three-step approach to help you spend less:

Step 1: Cut out the Fat

You completed your income and outgoings on page 70 and I want you to look at this again. What can you apply from the money saving tips that I have just listed to your outgoings? What can you do without, don't use, or give up altogether?

Now, let me be clear again, I don't want you to give up things that you like, please keep them. I simply want you to 'trim the fat' so to speak. What area of your spending can you target and focus on that will help improve your outgoings each month?

Before you identify some areas that you are wasting your money on, let me try and help you with this process. I want you to ask yourself when you look at your outgoings the following questions:

- Do I really need to be paying this expense anymore?
- If I give it up, will my overall happiness be less, i.e. am I happier with this particular expense?
- Would it feel good to get rid of this expense?
- What areas can I give up or at least cut back on that would not drastically affect my well-being?

OK, let's have a look at those outgoings again but this time I am going to include two more columns and show you an example of how this might look like in action using just some typical expenses.

Expense	Current Monthly Cost	New/Target Monthly Cost	Targeted saving
Food	€800	€750	€50
Clothing	€100	€50	€50
Insurance (life, home, health)	€200	€160	€40
Utilities (gas/electric/ phone etc.)	€180	€160	€20
Gym membership	€80	€0	€80
Savings	€0	€50	€50
Takeaways	€80	€55	€25
Entertainment	€50	€50	€0

Take your time when doing this exercise and record what you are actually spending each month and then calculate what you can realistically cut from each category, if you can cut anything at all. Don't over-promise yourself, because, if you discover after a month that you still spent the same amount as the month before then you will become disheartened. Don't go for the big saving in the first month, start small and see if this is realistic. Maybe there is no more to be cut and in that case, leave this expense alone and move on to the next.

Sometimes cutting back on what you are spending your money on is all you need to do to get your financial affairs in order. You may have to make some hard choices now if you want to become truly debt-free and financially secure. If you haven't been able to bring your expenses in line with what you earn each month, then the question is not whether you are going to have to make hard choices, but rather which hard choices you are going to make.

Now that you have identified areas that you may be able to improve on, there is a second way to improve your finances further.

Step 2: Shop Smart

I am not referring here to your weekly grocery shopping, I am talking about where you spend less than what you need to and still get the same value as you did before. What I want you to feel is that you are getting the absolute most out of your euro every time you spend it.

For example, can you reduce your health insurance premium by switching to a provider that tailors a plan to suit your needs?

I always come across people who pay so much more than they need to for life cover and in many cases they can lower their monthly premium and get more cover! Now that's shopping smart and getting bang for your buck.

Let's look at those fixed expenses that many of us take for granted and see if we improve on them. Before you do anything, I want you to ask and answer the following questions first:

- Am I really getting the best value for my money each month?

- What have I done to lower the price of this expense?

- Have I done my homework and compared the various providers in the marketplace?

What I want you to do for the following week is to break down each expense and review them one day at a time, rather than trying to tackle all of them at once. I want you to pick one expense, find out how much you are paying each month for it, review what you are covered for and then do your homework to see if you can make any improvements. This exercise may look something like this:

Day	Review
Monday	Home Insurance
Tuesday	Life Assurance
Wednesday	Health Insurance
Thursday	Car Loan
Friday	Car Insurance

Add in for the following week, review credit card and switch to a 0 percent provider, review telephone provider, review gas/electricity and so on.

A client of mine completed this exercise recently and she found that she could save €12.65 each month on her life policy, €19.63 on her home insurance monthly premium and she moved her car loan from her bank to her credit union saving herself €35 each month. She could not improve on her car or health insurance premiums. Whilst the savings where not life-changing amounts, she said all she needed was thirty minutes, a laptop and a phone – it was that easy. So please make the time to review what you are paying and take nothing for granted.

Step 3: Spend with the Long Term in Mind

This for me is going to be the best way to stop you spending your money on the things you don't want. If you want to spend money each month on big car loan payments or on cigarettes or whatever it is, think of the long-term impact of what you are doing. I had big car loan payments on a fancy car but I also had three young kids who I have to put through college, so for me it was easy to spend my money on savings rather than on a car.

A client of mine was paying €42 for life cover when all he needed to pay was €10 each month and when you look at what that saving of €32 each month could do for him in the long run, it could have:

- Reduced the term on his mortgage by eighteen months if applied as overpayment
- Accumulated €4,623 in a savings plan over ten years
- Added €51,437 to his pension plan when he retired

He never thought that €32 each month could take eighteen months off his mortgage and what's more, this was not costing him any extra each month, he was just using what he was already paying but doing it in a much better way.

Successful people focus on the long term and they have a vision for what the money they spend will become. This is not being miserly, this is being smart and looking after their money, you should do the same thing.

Let me quote one of my favourite authors here, Jim Rohn, who said: 'The philosophy of the rich versus the poor is this: The rich invest their money and spend what's left; the poor spend their money and invest what's left; it's the same money.'

OK, I have focused on the areas that you can cut back on and get better value for, but how about increasing your income – can this be done?

Yeah right, at a time of recession, sorry depression, this guy is talking about increasing your income when there have never been so many people unemployed and emigrating? Yes, I am, because whether you are employed or unemployed, there are things that you can do to improve your finances. It's all down to you.

Liam's Action List

- A little can go a long way. Review what your fixed monthly outgoings are costing you. Don't assume you can't get better value elsewhere.

- How much money do you spend each month on entertainment? Things like evenings out, shows, sporting events and so on. I have seen that this kind of spending has a way of growing out of control over time. Maybe now is the chance to review this and cut back? For example, instead of going out twice a week, maybe make it once.

- Lowering the interest rate charged on a loan or credit card can make a big impact on the total amount of interest you have to pay back over the life of a loan. Check with your credit card provider in particular to see if they will lower the interest rate they charge you. If they won't and you have a good credit rating, then move immediately to a provider who is offering a lower rate. You could even get a rate of 0 percent!

- Cut out bad habits – whether it's alcohol or cigarettes, if you use a lot of either then you know how expensive bad habits can be. If you find can't stop completely, think about cutting back and using the savings toward your other expenses. You'll see your bills come down – and feel your health improve – in no time. You'll also save on health care expenses down the road, and you may become eligible for lower insurance premiums.

- Cut back, not out. Rather than cutting out an expense altogether, maybe buy it less often.

- Small steps. Don't try and achieve big savings over a short space of time. You must tackle these savings in baby steps, so reduce what you have to do down into daily tasks. Set yourself a task on Day 1 to see if you can get one of your fixed expenses at a cheaper rate or price. If this takes you two minutes or two hours, don't take on any new tasks for that day. On Day 2, identify another fixed expense that you are going to check into, and so on. Rome wasn't built in a day and neither will you be able to improve your cash flow in one day either, so take it one day at a time.

'Do not wait to strike until the iron is hot; but make it hot by striking.'

–William B. Sprague

08

How You Can Increase Your Income

I am now going to give you some ideas for increasing your income that apply whether you are in or out of a job.

The Wacky World of Business – Now it's Your Turn!

Yes, the pace and severity of the economic crash that we are currently experiencing has caught all of us by surprise. More and more people are being made redundant each and every day and it seems that no one, no matter what profession or how skilled or qualified they are, is immune from this recession.

What would you think if I said that most people plan on becoming poor? It's true that when people speak about retiring they say confidently that their income will go down. In other words, they planned on working hard all of their lives only to become poorer.

The majority of people who are fortunate to have a job at present are actually planning on becoming poorer as they get older and they are happy and content with this happening to them. Maybe you were one of these people before you were made or might be made redundant? This certainly focuses the mind and makes people think differently about their career and where they would like to see it end up. It makes people more determined to rise to the challenge and say 'I am not going to let this happen to me'.

In the US, for example, research conducted by the Department of Health, Education and Welfare, tracking people from age twenty to sixty-five, found that by age sixty-five for every 100 people:

- 36 were dead
- 54 were living off the state-sponsored old age pension
- 5 were still working because they had to
- 4 were well-off
- 1 was wealthy

Maybe out of this adversity that we find ourselves in today, you will decide not to become one of those fifty-four people who has to rely on the state for income in their sixties. You now decide to become one of those five people who are well-off, or wealthy even, from your present position of debt.

So, how are you going to do this and what needs to be done?

Remember – wealth is all around you

Every day people who are not as smart as you are making money in every kind of business you can think of. Take a look around you, just about everything you can see right now is the result of a business that someone owns. Just about everything you use and consume was created, manufactured, sold, serviced or shipped by someone's business.

These days, with the internet, corporate downsizing and jobs being shipped overseas, it is both critical and crucial to consider starting your own business.

Now it's your turn!

I am not suggesting that you start a business from home or quit your day job if you have one because, as you will see, becoming your own boss is not easy. But you know what? It is not impossible either!

Just look at these examples:

There is a company that was set up in New York called 'Newyourkey'. For a small fee this company will keep a copy of your house or car key in a secure storage facility and can deliver them straight away if customers find themselves locked out. So, on the way home from a nightclub and can't find your keys? No problem, Newyourkey will deliver spare keys within an hour any time day or night.

Peasy.com is a company that allows people to search online for parking spaces before they leave home. So, if you own a car park space you could start earning money from it by adding it to the Peasy network.

So, you give your details, where your car park space is, when it is available and whether it can be rented weekly or monthly or both. People who then require parking can search online for suitable parking spaces.

This company identified the need people have to secure parking before they go on their journey. Parking in London, for example, is so difficult to get even with lots of car parks that their market research found that people would be willing to book a space before leaving home. Hence the reason this very successful and profitable company was formed.

Santamail: How is this for a great idea. Get a postal address at the North Pole, Alaska. Pretend you are St. Nick and charge $10 to parents for every letter you send to their kids from Santa. Founder, Byron Reese, has sent over 200,000 of these letters since 2001 and this simple idea has made him a couple of million dollars richer!

Fitdeck: Phil Black created a deck of cards featuring exercise routines and began selling it online for $18.95. It may sound like an unlikely business, but the former Navy SEAL and fitness instructor reported sales last year of $4.7 million!

The myths about being in business for yourself

To begin with, let's talk about some of the many myths that discourage people from even considering going into business for themselves. Separating the facts from the fiction can totally transform your attitude.

Myth No. 1: You need a lot of money to start

The reality for most small businesses is that starting them takes less money than you think. The average start-up cost for some of the fastest growing small businesses was €25,000 and many of them were started with €5,000 or less.

Myth No. 2: You need to have experience

Friends and relatives will warn you that you need to have experience in business to be able to start one. Don't let these people discourage you, even if they are just looking after your best interests.

Experience certainly does help but action beats inaction any day of the week. Besides, you do not have to go it alone; there are many resources available to you which will make you wonder why you waited so long to start. There are countless companies that can help you get your business off the ground with training and mentoring systems that are designed to help you succeed.

Franchising, for example, is a very popular way of building on an existing business and has proven to be very successful for many people. Today, the franchising industry is everything. It's the auctioneering firm you bought your house from, the coffee shop, hotels, pet grooming salons, computer training courses and much more.

Myth No. 3: Nine out of ten new businesses fail

This much heralded statistic does not match up with what is happening in the real world. Statistically, nearly two-thirds of all new businesses survive at least two years with about half surviving until at least year four.

Myth No. 4: You need a lot of 'stuff' to get started

I have spoken with several entrepreneurs, wealthy, self-made people who all say the same thing – the only things you absolutely need to start a business are passion, commitment, desire and a willingness to take action. I personally know of a businessman who generates €1 million in annual revenue without having an office, a business plan, business cards or stationary – what he does have is passion and commitment.

Myth No.5: You have to be passionate about the particular business you choose

Many people are held back by this cliché because they believe that 'what they love' will not make money or they just don't know what they love or are passionate about. If your goal is to earn €5,000 per month, that in itself can be enough reason to start your own business. 'Profits are better than wages. Wages make you a living; profits make you a fortune' (Jim Rohn).

Myth No. 6: You are too old or young to start

When I speak with people who feel that they are too old to start a business I ask them have they read the story of Colonel Sanders of KFC fame, who did not start to become rich and successful until he was in his late sixties. Women often say that it's a man's world, but read the story of Anita Roddick, founder of the Body Shop, or Muriel Schiefer, the first women to have a seat on the New York stock exchange, to help inspire and change your mind. When people say they are too young, read about Bill Gates, who became the richest man in the world in his early thirties.

What sort of an employee are you?

There are so many people being made redundant these days it is starting to feel like a case of who's next? I think everyone knows someone who has been let go in the past few months; can anything be done to protect you from becoming the next person to join the dole queue?

The answer really is yes and no. Certainly, there are external factors that will be beyond your control, but there are things you can do to help yourself. You can start by learning the '20/60/20 Principle'.

Let me explain. If you are an employee, you can go to work, do your job and get what you get. Alternatively, you can go to work with an action plan and create a future for yourself, it is really one or the other!

Over the years, business leaders and owners have noticed the same thing at just about every workplace – employees seem to break down into three basic groups: 20 percent fall into the bottom group, 60 percent into the middle group and 20 percent are in the top group.

Bottom 20 percent have no clue

The people in this group barely get to work on time; they are employed or in business in spite of themselves. They have little or no interest in how the company is performing and work just for their weekly pay cheque. They don't seek job satisfaction and view any of their co-workers who express an interest in advancement with distain.

Middle 60 percent want a clue

Most employees are good people and want to get on and do well. They are hardworking, honest and doing a job they are supposed to do. They try and work hard but for some, life never seems easy. They would like to advance in their workplace and some would like to change their careers altogether. They just don't know how to go about this and some are even afraid to ask. They sometimes lack that initiative or spark that would move them onto the next level.

Top 20 percent have a clue

These employees know that you only get what you go for. They come to work with a specific career and income goal. The take ownership and manage the direction of their lives. They know how to influence people and consider themselves winners. You can see this in how they dress, talk, act and live. They have purpose and meaning.

Now let me ask you a question that you probably know the answer to already – which category do you belong to? By the way, your family, friends, co-workers and most importantly your boss also know this answer.

If you don't like the image of yourself, then change! Most people have lived in all three categories and will tell you that the air is certainly better in the top 20 percent.

You can't get to the top 20 percent simply by wishing and hoping, you have to make a plan and then act on it.

The Pareto Principle

Back in 1906 an Italian economist named Vilfredo Pareto noticed that 20 percent of the Italian people owned 80 percent of Italy's total wealth. This has become known as the 80-20 rule which simply means that 20 percent of what you do accounts for 80 percent of your results. In other words 80 percent of your effort really does not matter that much.

So, if you are going to become a more valuable employee, you have to move into the top 20 percent and figure out which of your efforts account for most of the value you add to your job. If you can do this you will become an employee that your boss or employers will view as indispensible; and if they are looking at making cuts and redundancies you want to be the one person they could not do without!

There are many other ways to increase your income, such as renting out a room, working more hours (if you can), taking on a second job, working overtime (again, if you can) or asking for a pay rise. A pay rise? Are you absolutely joking? No I am not. Did you read what I said about becoming a better employee?

If you do choose this option, think about it first. Make a list of all of the reasons you deserve a raise, don't simply say to your boss 'I need more money', you need to convince him/her that you are worth the extra investment based on what you offer the company, not on what you personally need.

Remember this fantastic quote from Jim Rohn: 'Your paycheck is not your employer's responsibility, it's your responsibility. Your employer has no control over your value, but you do.'

Liam's Action List

- Commit to becoming a better and more valuable employee. Remember this: your employer doesn't just pay you an hourly wage for nothing, it pays you an hourly rate for what value you bring to the company for that hour. The more value you bring, the more you will get paid.

- Are there new sources of income that you can earn aside from your day job? What are you good at doing that people would pay you for?

- Can you create a new business from your own home? Have you an idea that you think would make a great business and could be done from home? Do some research, and see if people would pay you for this product or service you have. What have you got to lose? Don't seek advice from friends or family for the time being because they will just put you off, so put in the hard work yourself and seek expert advice. Don't just think about it, do it.

- Regardless of what age you are, don't think for a moment that you are either too young or too old. That is just nonsense. If the idea is good enough and you are committed enough, you will succeed. As Dale Carnegie once said, 'Today is life – the only life you are sure of. Make the most of today. Let the winds of enthusiasm sweep through you. Live today with gusto.'

- Work on yourself before you work on anything else. Take some classes if you need to, to enhance your skills or develop new ones. Learning and improving will boost everything about you, making you feel better, and when you feel better, you achieve more.

- Make sure you claim all you are entitled to. Claiming for tax reliefs is an area that still surprises me because of the large number of people who neglect claiming for things they are entitled to. There are hundreds of millions of euros that go unclaimed each year by every one of us, so familiarise yourself with what you may be entitled to and make your claim.

'There's no telling what you can do when you get inspired by them. There's no telling what you can do when you believe in them. And there's no telling what will happen when you act upon them.'

–Jim Rohn

09

Goal Setting

It has been said that there are three kinds of people:

- Those that make things happen
- Those who let things happen
- Those who wonder what happened

We fit into each of these categories at various times in our lives. However, when it comes to your finances, you really want to be the one in control . . . you want to be in the group that makes things happen.

Do you ever start daydreaming, thinking about how your life is and how you wish it was? Almost everyone, poor or wealthy, wants to do something that will change their life. No matter what it is you want to change, whether it is something to do with your family life, work life or your finances, the first step is setting yourself goals.

When I give presentations and I start talking about goals and goal setting, I can see by the looks on the faces in the audience that 99.9 percent of them do not set goals. Some people even find it hard to come up with a financial goal they would like to achieve and they wonder why they struggle financially.

What happens at the beginning of each year? We announce our New Year's resolutions, which are another way of setting out the goals we would like to achieve in the coming year. We promise ourselves that we are going to do this or that, we buy the same money-advice books that we bought the year before, which give us the basic information, and before March arrives, you won't be able to tell me what your resolutions were in the first place. You are no better off than you were a few months previous.

I am going to show you what goal setting is and how important it can be in helping you improve your financial well-being. I will show you how it can, and will, get you out of debt and how it increases your motivation to follow through on what you promised yourself.

Goal setting is the simple process of personal planning. By setting goals, you decide what you want to achieve and then move in a step-by-step manner towards achieving it.

Goal setting is a standard technique used by professional athletes, successful business people and high achievers. You can be sure that Padraig Harrington at the start of each golfing year sets goals and targets for himself that he wants to reach. He then goes about planning, training, learning and practising until those goals are achieved. It isn't by luck or chance that he wins golf tournaments. Yes, he is fantastically gifted at what he does, but he is constantly striving, focused and determined that he will achieve his goals and won't settle for just ordinary results; he wants fantastic results, he wants to win more majors, he wants to win the order of merit every year, he wants to play in the Ryder Cup. Padraig Harrington doesn't *hope* he wins golf tournaments, he expects to win every single one.

The same principles apply to your finances. If you don't have financial goals, then you don't have a plan and if you don't have a plan you have no idea what you want to achieve. If you are travelling by car to a city or town you never visited before, do you get into your car and drive aimlessly around hoping you will magically arrive? Of course not, you plan your trip in advance, you look at what route to take and how long it will take you to get there, so even before you leave you know where you are going. Are you starting to see the importance of having financial goals?

I was working with a company recently who were going through a compulsory redundancy programme, and they asked me to come in and help those who were being made redundant. Each person I met was obviously very upset and worried about their future and particularly concerned about their finances. When would they get another job, how will they be able to meet their mortgage payments if they don't, etc.

It was difficult for everybody because one after the other, the same worries and concerns came up. However, one guy I met bounced into the meeting room to see me. Outwardly he seemed in great form. How are things I asked? Great came his reply. Really? Are you not concerned or worried? You just lost your job. Not really, he said, yes it was disappointing that the factory was closing but what can you do? Great attitude, I thought, so let's get stuck into your finances I said. Who is your mortgage with? I don't have a mortgage, came the reply along with a huge smile across his face. This gentleman told me that when he borrowed the equivalent of €250,000 fifteen years ago, he made it his goal that he was going to have that paid and be mortgage-free by the time he was forty-one. He was going to overpay on his mortgage each month, he was going to use any salary increase that came his way to use against his mortgage and any bonus he received would be paid against his mortgage rather than partly financing a new car or going on a second holiday that year. He didn't clear his mortgage at forty-one, but he did at forty-three – his goal was to become mortgage free as fast as possible and rather than hoping this became a reality, he made it become a reality.

All of us who have mortgages would like to be mortgage free but what do we do about turning this dream into a reality? How many of us even find out how this can be achieved? Very few I suspect.

If your goal is to be debt-free, how are you going to achieve this? What are your goals? What do you want to achieve financially? What do you want to spend your money on to help achieve these goals?

Let's start off with some generic goals first. List ten goals that require money. Call this list 'Things I Want That Require Money'; it might look something like this:

1. I want to clear my credit card debt
2. I want to save money to go on holidays next year
3. I want to become mortgage free
4. I want to save more for retirement
5 . I want to save for a deposit on a house
6. I want to save enough money to put my children through college
7. I want to save for my wedding
8. I want to save more money each month
9. I want to spend less than I earn
10. I want to become debt-free

I hope the above suggestions will give you an example of just some financial goals that various people I have met over the past number of years have.

When setting your financial goals, it is helpful to separate your goals into different time periods, i.e. short-term goals (these should take you less than two years to achieve) and long-term goals (anywhere between two and five years).

The 5-Step Approach to Achieving your Goals

1. Prioritise Your Goals

The first step in prioritising your goals is deciding if something is absolutely needed or is it something you simply want. A need is a necessity and a want is something you would like but is not absolutely necessary.

When setting goals, should you prioritise saving money first for a new car over saving for your retirement? Of course you shouldn't, so you need to always ask yourself this question when looking at what your goals are.

2. Make your goals SMART

Setting goals for the sake of it and just coming up with things you would like to achieve is just a wish list, nothing more and nothing will ever come of it, I assure you. You have to define exactly what your goals are and what you want to achieve, so I have put together five qualities that will help you to clarify exactly what your goals are:

S – Specific – what is the result you want to achieve? Be very specific, goals like 'I want to make more money' sound fine but they are too vague. By answering specifically how much you want to make, you can be more detailed about setting your goal – e.g. 'I want to make €20,000 in the next six months' – that is a very detailed, specific goal.

M – Measureable – What is a successful result? How will you know if you have achieved your goal? When setting financial goals, measuring it is easy because there is a number associated with the goal, and you have something to measure against and track how you are doing.

A – Achievable – Yes you should set your goals high but you also have to be realistic. 'I want to retire at fifty-five on an income of €65,000 per year' sounds good, it's even measureable and specific but how achievable is it? You have to balance between pushing yourself to accomplish a goal and making them realistic.

If you set yourself a goal of getting rid of your €10,000 credit card debt in six months, but your earnings are less than €30,000 per year, you will not be successful in getting rid of this debt in that time frame, so keep your goals simple, manageable and achievable.

R – Realistic – A realistic goal is one that will stretch you but that is not impossible to achieve. Cutting out completely on all entertainment and eating or having a few drinks out at weekends might not be realistic for most, but starting to reduce the amount of money spent in these areas might be.

T – Trackable – What is your cut-off date for achieving your goal? There has to be a finish line so that you push yourself to achieve your goal. Without a timeline for completing your goal, it is very easy to get off track.

Remember, a goal without a deadline is just a wish!

When I work with individuals on a one-to-one basis, we sit down and factor in all of the above areas when determining what goal it is they want to achieve. We are very specific, the goal is attainable and within their ability and, if they stick to their plan, they will be able to see the progress they are making.

Before they even start putting their plan into place, we have their 'Debt Freedom Day' identified. They know exactly what day they will become debt-free, or the exact day their chosen goal or specific debt will be cleared. I normally get them to put this day somewhere visible like on the fridge door so it is something they can see and will be a constant reminder of what all the hard work is about.

The same applies to a goal of saving for a holiday. For example, cutting out a picture of the resort you are going to in twelve months' time and having that somewhere you can see it will motivate you to keep saving and prevent you from taking the easy way out and putting it on your credit card or taking out a personal loan.

3. Create an action plan

What I want you to do is write down your goals again, but this time rather than listing lots of them, I want you to list your top three. Now they could be short- or long-term, it really doesn't matter, now let's apply the SMART principle to them.

Top 3 Values	Top 3 Financial Goals	Be specific and measurable	48 Hour Plan – what actions do you need to take in the next 48 hours?	Enlist help – who will help you achieve your goals?	Start and Finish Line – When will you start and when will you finish?
Security	Reduce term on mortgage	Overpay mortgage each month and change frequency of payment	Call to bank and set up standing order for extra €100 each month	Speak with advisor about benefits of paying every two weeks rather than once a month	Starting 1 May 2012, mortgage will be repaid in full on 19 January 2019
Giving my child the best education they can get	Pay for children's third level education	The cost is going to be c. €35,000, my child is now nine and I will need this amount in ten years' time	Call to bank and set up a regular savings account in the amount of €250 per month	Speak with member of staff in bank to see if there are accounts that are suitable for this long-term savings plan – what are the best interest rates they can offer?	Starting on the 10 July 2012, I will have €34,797.25 in my account on the 10 July 2022
I want to become my own boss	Clear credit card debt of €5,000	Before I can start my own business I need to clear my credit card debt	Increase standing order from €125 per month to €250 per month	See if you can transfer card to a 0 percent provider if you can, if not doesn't matter	Starting on the 1 August 2012, my credit card debt will be cleared in full on the 1 September 2014

Can you remember when I listed ten typical goals that people strive to achieve but never do because all they do is write these dreams down and never do anything about them? Can you see from the last couple of pages that if you want to achieve your goals, you have to put a plan in place and do something about it and if you do, you will achieve them, this I guarantee you!

Here is an example of this in action for a client of mine who had two short-term wishes that I turned into goals.

Short-Term Money Goals (2012)

Priority	Description	Action to be taken	Target date for completion	Cost estimate	Savings needed per month
1	Change car	Set up direct debit from current account	1 September	€2,000	€250
2	Holiday	Set up direct debit from current account	1 November	€1,800	€200

Here is another example of a client who had some more medium-term goals in mind, he wrote them down and this is what they looked like:

Priority	Description	Action to be taken	Target date for completion	Target	Savings needed per month
1	Emergency Fund	Set up direct debit from current account	1 February 2015	€9,000	€250
2	Repayment of Personal Loan	Set up standing order from current account	1 October 2015	€9,200	€200
3	Pay off Credit Card Completely	Set up standing order from current account	1 September 2012	€600	€100

4. Get organised

If you want to reach your goals, you will need to be able to track your financial affairs.

I normally recommend two systems for people, which are paper records or electronic records. You could, of course, use a combination of both. Whatever works best for you is fine, but the important thing about this is recording and filing your information in a way that is easily retrievable and easily found. If putting all Visa statements in a shoe box marked 'Visa Statements 2012' works for you, then that's fine with me.

It is also very important that you schedule your time each week or month to stay on top of your goals and to review how you are doing. Make it something that you do at a particular time each week or month where you spend ten minutes updating your information, assessing how you are doing and planning what you are going to do in the week ahead.

5. Keep it real

Hopefully by reviewing your outgoings and writing down what goals you want to achieve, you have discovered areas that exist in your financial life that need improvement. Mortgage and loan repayments are the obvious barriers to creating any wealth or having a bigger cash flow surplus for people and these are the areas that they need to focus on most.

However, a word of caution. I always find with clients that if they are not realistic with their goals, they only set themselves up for failure and discouragement down the road. The main reasons goals fail are because people:

- Have unrealistic expectations
- Don't have a written plan

The very essence of having financial goals is that you want achieve something else in your life. Having a goal of becoming mortgage-free, for example, is not the overriding reason you are striving to achieve this. The reason might be that you hate your job but you cannot do anything about that because you need a monthly paycheque to pay the bank and keep the roof over your head. The reason for having no mortgage is because you can then go and pursue your dreams – this is the reason I want you to put down what your values are when you are applying the SMART principles.

I met a person recently whose number one goal was to save for their child's education. When I quizzed him on why this was so important, I discovered that as a child his parents were not in a position to help him go to college. So while all his friends went off and got degrees and had a great time in university, he worked in a shop. There is nothing wrong with working in a shop and he has turned out much more successful than many of his friends who went to college, and he employs many hundreds of people himself, but he still has that anxiety that he does not want what happened to him to happen to his own child. That was his motivation and that was why he was going to achieve his goal.

You see, I think if your reason is strong enough, then you will have no difficulty in achieving your goals, but occasionally you will encounter some obstacles in reaching them. Therefore, anticipate having to make adjustments and find ways around them, and don't lose sight of the things you value most in life. If, at one stage, you have a particular goal that you wanted to achieve and then it becomes something that is no longer important to you, then let go of it. This will allow you to focus on other goals that may become important to you.

Let me again state that the value of setting and writing down what your goals are cannot be over-emphasized. They start as a dream, but with a plan in place, and with your desire and drive, you can make them a reality. And by understanding why you want them to become a reality, you will have a better chance of reaching them.

Let me give you six tips that helped me reach my goals:

- Always keep the most important goals in the forefront of your mind.

- Write your goals down and post them on the fridge including the dates you want to achieve them by – write in big bold letters your 'Debt Freedom Day'.

- Keep your goals in your wallet or purse as well, so that if you are ever tempted to waste your money on something you don't really need, and you are tempted to use credit to purchase it, your goals will be a constant reminder to think twice.

- Keep them realistic – if your circumstances change, i.e. you lose your job, your income is reduced, you suffer an illness, you get married, you become a parent, you get separated or whatever it is, then re-asses your situation.

- Your previous goals may become unrealistic or not as important now, so you may have to change them, be flexible.

- Always have short- and long-term goals. If you only ever have long-term goals, they may seem forever and a day away, so make sure you have some goals that are short in duration and that can be achieved in less than two years.

Liam's Action List

- List your financial goals in order of priority, with the most important ones coming first. Divide these goals into short-, medium- and long-term goals.

- Make your goals Specific, Measureable, Achievable, Realistic and Trackable (SMART).

- Work out what resources you have at your disposal and what you will need in order to achieve each goal.

- Assign deadlines for each goal and put them onto a calendar that you normally look at each day.

- Communicate your goals with your partner and /or a trusted friend. Communicating regularly with someone about your goals helps maintain your focus and keeps you motivated

- As Jim Rohn said, 'If you go to work on your goals, they will go to work on you.' And as I say, 'An unwritten goal is just a wish. When you see what you want and you want it bad enough, you will find a way to get it.' Write down your goals and get working on making them become a reality.

- In order to visualise your goals and stay motivated, you need to set daily goals. And these can and should be very simple, like making that phone call, or just reminding yourself what your goals actually are. In addition to keeping you on track, it will keep pushing and pushing you to achieve your goals.

- Look at your goals every day. Write down your goals and put them in your wallet or on your fridge door, some place that you will see them every day. One of my goals is to own a property in Florida with no mortgage, so what do you think is on my fridge in my home? Yes, you got it, a big picture of an amazing house with a pool in Orlando, Florida. Every day it reminds me of why I do what I do and what I am going to have in the next ten years.

'Don't stretch yourself too much with a mortgage. Buy within your means, it's not worth the sleepless nights.'

–Sarah Beeny

10

How to Take Ten Years Off Your Mortgage

I am now going to show you what you can do to get yourself out of the debt you are currently in. I will focus on those areas of debt that are common to most people, and demonstrate what can be done to rid yourself of it, saving you thousands in the process.

Let's start off with the biggest debt of all, your mortgage.

Imagine for a moment that you are writing the last cheque to your mortgage lender and all your debts are now paid off. You feel the weight of all this debt lift from your shoulders. You're free! Now what are you going to do? Vacation? Spend more time with loved ones? Retirement planning that you can now afford?

Now what if this dream could be a reality?

A survey was carried out recently and the single biggest thing that people felt would change their lives for the better was paying off their home loan and becoming mortgage free.

'Yeah, if only', I can hear you say, 'I am up to my eyes in negative equity, it's impossible'. But it can be achieved; becoming mortgage free can be done by real people like you and me.

The possibility of being in debt forever has become a real prospect for some homeowners, particularly with falling house prices, higher-than-ever mortgage amounts, interest-only loans and so on. It has resulted in huge loans that we grudgingly spend most of our adult lives repaying.

The term 'mortgage' has its origins in France and literally translates into English as 'death contract'. For many people that is exactly what it is – a legally binding contract that will not end until you are close to death!

The Irish regard their home as their castle and therefore the offer of a mortgage on a house is a cause for celebration. We view our home as an asset when, of course, it is not; it is the biggest, most expensive loan you will ever take on. The quicker it is repaid in full the better-off financially you will be and the better your quality of life will become.

'That's great, Liam, but unless we win the lottery, repaying a mortgage of say €400,000 in less than twenty years will be beyond our means, as well as the willpower of most borrowers. You could work eight days a week and live off baked beans until your loan is cleared, but for the majority of us this is unrealistic.

But what if you were mortgage free? What if you didn't have that monthly burden, which is actually lining your bank's pockets?

A mortgage is set up to drain your bank account and people don't realise that they are, in fact, working for their bank! Banks know that you could repay your mortgage much faster than the terms on which it is agreed, but they are not going to tell you how or help you in because it cuts their ability to take your money for years on end.

So, a bank wants you to keep paying them for decades, but what if you repaid your mortgage in a fraction of the time? What if you could say, 'goodbye money worries'?

Because many people have very high mortgages, they are unable to set aside money for their retirement. They just don't have it, so they rely on the state old-age pension as their only source of income in retirement – they actually plan on getting poorer as they get older. This is unfortunately becoming a fact of life for many people nowadays.

On 5 January 2006 a young couple were interviewed by the BBC on how they managed to pay off their mortgage in two years.

They had set themselves a goal of paying off their mortgage early so they could give up their jobs and move to mainland Europe. So, how did they achieve their goal? By both saving and making money.

He, for example, gave up his season ticket to his local football club, she gave up cigarettes, and they both cut back on drink, takeaways and so on. This alone was not going to repay their mortgage but they showed determination and enterprise in making extra money.

This couple were told by friends that there was no way they could pay off their mortgage in two years but they ignored this advice and focused on their dream, which was freedom to leave their jobs and find a new dream life abroad. They showed a huge belief in their ability to achieve this goal and they were successful.

There are many other examples of people who decided to try and become mortgage-free and before you dismiss this as an unrealistic option, and put up your circumstances as a defence (or excuse), let me state something. Another couple who achieved their goal had two pre-school kids, and they earned an average wage. She did not work as she wanted to stay at home with the kids. They were not wealthy, but with determination and some simple-to-follow strategies they succeeded – so it can be done!

The big obstacle that people have to overcome is their thinking. As a financial coach I have spent thousands of hours helping families get in control of their finances and teaching them how to overcome their debt. In every single situation I can promise you the very first obstacle we have to surmount is their head-space.

OK, so why would you want to be mortgage-free? Here are a few reasons:

Freedom – Can you imagine the freedom of not having that mortgage repayment hanging over your head each month? Now you would only have to earn enough to pay for basic necessities.

Imagine the possibilities this could open for you. You could afford to quit your job and start a business, travel, help your children financially – *the world is your oyster!*

Less Stress – Not having a mortgage repayment would mean significantly less stress in your life. You wouldn't have to worry as much about losing your job, for example.

Liquidity – What I mean here is that if, for example, your mortgage payment is €1,500 per month and if you could pay it off, you would have an extra €1,500 in your bank account. You could invest this and when you reach old age become one of those people in the 5 percent bracket that I mentioned earlier!

Safety – Once your mortgage is finished then you truly own your home. This, without pointing out the obvious, means you always have a place to go to. You can't live in a stock market certificate! Owning your own home is a safe investment for the simple reason that you always have a shelter.

Reducing Loan Stress – Paying off your mortgage early also reduces loan-related stress. Houses, as we know, gain and lose value and these market changes affect the equity you have built up in your home. Without a loan you remove the risk of negative equity. You also avoid being hit by climbing interest rates.

There are many thousands of people now in a negative equity situation and they feel helpless. But what can you do about it?

Let me give you a quick example of how I took ten years off a mortgage for a couple withou making any significant impact on their lives. It was a three-pronged attack but so simple.

Number 1 – 'The 'Latte Factor'

First off, did you know that by cutting back on some luxury items you would save the following against a €300,000 mortgage over a thirty-year term?

- Sports TV Subscription
  1 year 5 months off your mortgage and €12,569 in interest savings

- 10 Cigarettes per day
  3 years 9 months off your mortgage and €31,660 in interest

- 1 Cappuccino per day
  2 years off your mortgage and €16,606 in interest savings

- 1 Chocolate bar per day
  8 months off your mortgage and €6,487 in interest savings

Can you believe what an impact such small changes could have on your overall finances?

Number 2 – The bi-weekly repayment plan

The second way to become debt-free is an industry secret. It is simply using a bi-weekly payment plan to pay down your mortgage and doing it automatically. Instead of making a monthly repayment the way you are currently doing, you split it down the middle and pay half every two weeks.

If you had a mortgage of €300,000 at say 4 percent over a thirty-year period, then this loan will cost you €215,608 in interest charges over the life of the loan. On a bi-weekly basis, the same mortgage will cost you a total of just €181,950 in interest.

In other words, switching to this simple method of repayment you will save more than €33,657 in interest payments and take four years off the term of your mortgage. A hugely beneficial change that takes five minutes to do.

Some banks do not encourage or want you to make your repayments like this, why? The basic reason is obvious – money.

Number 3 – Monthly overpayment

The third method of repaying your mortgage in a much faster time period is achieved by making an overpayment each month on top of your current repayment. If, for example, your mortgage balance was €300,000 and you overpaid by an extra €120 each month, doing this would reduce the term outstanding by four years, one months (saving over €33,549 in interest payments).

Could you find an extra €4 each day that could be applied to your mortgage?

Remember earlier in the book I spoke about how much you earn on an hourly basis and would you buy a pair of shoes if it you had to work for half a day to pay for them? Well this is much easier; all we have to find here is €4 each day.

If you are earning €30,000, it means that your hourly rate is about €15 before taxes, based on a forty-hour working week. This means that every minute you work, you earn €0.25 cent. So, all you have to work to achieve this €4 every day, is dedicate or pledge that the amount you earn for just *sixteen minutes* of your work every day is going towards your mortgage overpayment.

Based on a forty-hour working week, you will work 480 minutes every day. Can you spare sixteen minutes of them? And if you can increase your value to your employer, you can potentially earn even more money and will have to work less and less for that extra €4.

What I am showing you here is that with a combination of a regular overpayment, an adjustment to how frequently you repay your mortgage, and cutting back on small everyday items, that thirty-year, €300,000 mortgage can be paid off in ten years less, saving you around €83,812 in interest repayments in the process!

I have taught these principles to many hundreds of my clients over the past decade and I am glad to say that all of them are on track to repaying their mortgage in a much faster time frame than they even imagined.

Why not join them?

Liam's Action List

• Robert Kiyosaki, author of *Rich Dad Poor Dad*, was absolutely right when he said that your home is not an asset, it is a liability. An asset is something that puts money into your pocket, a liability is something that takes money out of it, which is exactly what a mortgage is.

- Look at the advantages of paying your mortgage twice a month, rather than once a month, or if this doesn't suit, pay one extra payment at the end of the year. Doing this could take years off the term of your mortgage.

- Can you overpay even a small amount each month on your mortgage? Look at your budget and find areas that you can save money on and then apply it as an overpayment on your mortgage. I worked with one client who was able to divert an extra €200 per month towards her mortgage which reduced her remaining term from thirty-two years to twenty-four.

- Repaying your mortgage as fast as you can will substantially reduce the amount of interest you will pay over time. If one of your goals is to move house in the next five years, then nothing will get you there faster than building up equity in your existing house. Equally, if you are in negative equity, nothing will get you out of it faster than overpaying on your mortgage each month.

- If you have a tracker mortgage and you have surplus funds left over each month, or you can find savings in other areas of your finances, then use the opportunity of the current low interest rate to overpay. They won't stay this low forever so take advantage now.

'Dear Santa, please send your credit card numbers. It's only fair since you're getting the credit for the gifts, that you should start paying for them also.'

–Unknown

11

The Credit Card Industry's Secret

You can throw the reminders in the bin, or even shred that envelope without even opening it because you already know its contents, right? You have had that phone call already, probably a message left on your answering machine, reminding you of how much you owe and that you are late with your monthly payment. Sound familiar? Of course it does. Credit card debt is a major problem in this country. While not everyone has a credit card, those that do typically carry a balance. The interest rate on a credit card balance is usually somewhere between 13-23 percent APR.

Credit card debt hovers like a carrion bird over a dying beast, with annual interest rates of up to 23 percent compounding month after month. Unfortunately, you can't just wish it away, but you can pay it down with determination. Before I show you how this can be done, let me share a secret the credit card industry doesn't want you to know about!

Curious? Any ideas? Well the answer is not what you might think! The secret simply is this: Credit card companies *want* you to take your time repaying them – in fact the longer you take, the happier they are!

Why? Because the longer you take the more interest you pay.

They don't really need you to pay off your debt in full – their profits go up when you only make minimum payments. They are smart enough to know that if they keep the minimum payment down low enough you will keep spending money and they will make a fortune on you.

They don't want you to know that if you have a debt of €1,000, for example, and you pay only the minimum payment each month at 18 percent, then it will take you ninety-three months – yes, you read that correctly – ninety-three months, or eight years, to pay off a debt of just €1,000 in full.

To understand why a relatively simple process works it's important to understand how minimum payments work. Minimum payments are calculated as a percentage of the outstanding balance. That means as your card balance slowly decreases, so does your minimum payment. This is why it can take ten years or more to pay off even a small balance if you only make the minimum payment each month.

You have to remember that you cannot make progress on your debt if you continue this way; the majority of the money you are giving the credit card provider each month is not going to pay down your debt – it is going to pay the interest, so all that happens is that someone else gets richer and you stay in a hole.

Let me give you an example – I met a couple a few weeks back who owed €12,500 on two credit cards and were paying them at an average rate of 15 percent. Their minimum monthly repayment, which they could barely afford to make, was €250 – 2 percent of the outstanding balance. Of that amount, €150 was going on interest payments. So, nearly €2,000 each year was going just to service the interest portion of their debt!

I keep telling people, it is not the credit card debt that is killing us, it is the interest! Credit card providers are even happier when you are late with a payment because then they can add late fees on top of the interest charged (it is predicted that the credit card industry will make in excess of $20 billion in late fees and penalties this year). In Ireland for example, you have two fees – a late payment fee and an over-your-credit-limit fee. A late payment fee can be as much as €15.24 each month and over-your- limit-fee of €12.70.

Now retailers and even football clubs are getting in on the act by offering store cards or branded cards. They offer you discounts on items purchased if you use their credit card. So, you are up at the counter buying something for €500 and you are offered a 10 percent discount if you open up a store card – €50 off? Sounds like a great deal.

Then your bill arrives a month later and suddenly you have to pay the €450. You see this little figure alongside it of €10, which is the minimum repayment. Relieved, you pay the €10 and that's how the debt starts to grow – you keep paying the minimum payment.

So, you continue to make the minimum payment, and nearly five years later you have paid off the debt on something which more than likely is long gone.

Remember, you should only borrow money to become rich, you should not borrow money to look rich, which I think has happened in the last number of years. You must not lease your lifestyle because if you do, you are going to be permanently in debt for the rest of your life!

The five worst credit card mistakes you can make

I have found that over the past twenty years of dealing with people's finances, when it comes to credit card debt, the mistakes people have made in this area are by in large down to five things:

1. Making minimum-only payments

As I have explained, making the minimum payment on your credit card not only increases the amount of time it takes to pay off your balance, it also increases the amount of interest you pay on your credit card.

Let me give you an example of the right way to pay your credit card debt and the wrong way.

Stupid Sean versus Smart Sarah

Both Sean and Sarah owe €5,000 in credit card debt at a rate of 16 percent APR.

The Wrong Way

Stupid Sean		
His first payment is	Paying the minimum payment will take this long to pay off	Total amount of interest paid
€125	27 years, 3 months	€5,289.48

The Right Way

Smart Sarah pays twice the minimum monthly payment		
Her monthly payment is	Paying twice the minimum payment will take this long to pay off	Total amount of interest paid
€250	24 months	€854.46

I want to stress how bad it is to be paying minimum amounts each month, so I want to show you again how long it would take before your debt is repaid in full based on small and big amounts.

Let's say you buy:	Paying minimum payments it will take you this long to pay it off:	Total amount of Interest paid:
€250 phone	6 years, 3 months	€ 136.38
€1,500 computer	18 years, 8 months	€ 1,492.48
€10,000 furniture	31 years, 11 months	€10,713.78

It's important to note also, that if you invested that minimum payment that is going towards your €10,000 credit card debt and earned 4 percent, it would have amounted to about €81,451 in savings!

2. Paying late

If you are constantly late paying your bill, as well as being charged an over-your-limit fee, you could be paying as much as €324 in late fees each year which are added to the amount you already owe!

3. Ignoring your credit card billing statement

If you don't open your credit card billing statement, you risk missing your payment due date. You could also miss important announcements about changes to your credit card terms.

4. Maxing out your credit card

Charging your credit card balance up to your credit limit and beyond is dangerous to your wallet and your credit score.

Getting close to your credit limit puts you at risk for over-the-limit fees and charges when you exceed your credit limit.

5. Not knowing your credit card terms

Knowing how your credit card company handles late payments makes you more likely to pay your credit card bill on time.

Knowing your credit card term gives you more control over your credit card costs. Do you know, for example, that you could be paying for 'payment protection' and not even know about it?

Fighting back

OK, so whether you are thinking of getting a new card or have one already, here is what you should be doing:

Limit the amount of cards you have

Fewer cards make it easier to track the amounts you owe, repayment dates etc.

Avoid store cards

Unless you repay the amount due each month, they tend to charge higher rates than normal cards.

Pay off the balance in full each month

Spend only what you can afford to pay for that month – set a budget and give yourself some tough love!

Cut your own limit

If you have a card and are worried, cut your own limit. This is another way of stopping your spending. Reduce the limit to an amount you can afford to pay each month.

Transfer to 0 percent providers

Everything you pay each month is going to reduce the debt in full – nothing going on interest. If a provider is giving ten months at 0 percent then switch to them and after this period is over try switch to another provider who is offering 0 percent for another ten months– now you have nearly two years of paying no interest with the full amount each month coming off what you owe. Even if you cannot switch to a provider who is charging 0 percent, a small change to the interest rate you are being charged can make a big difference as the table below shows.

Decrease in interest	€1,000 debt over 1 year	€5,000 debt over 3 years	€10,000 debt over 5 years
1 percent	Save € 10	Save € 151	Save € 510
3 percent	Save € 30	Save € 463	Save € 1,592
5 percent	Save € 50	Save € 788	Save € 2,763
10 percent	Save €100	Save €1,655	Save € 6,105
18 percent	Save €180	Save €3,215	Save €12,877

Use savings to clear in full

If you have some savings that earn 2 percent and you have debts charged at 18 percent then use your savings to repay this debt. However, and this is a very big however, always leave some money on deposit as your emergency fund; use your 'surplus' money, if you have any, to pay down on your debt.

Use prepaid credit cards

Using prepaid credit cards means you can never overspend and never get into debt. You can use or spend only what you put into them.

Switching card providers

If you have decided to switch to a new credit card provider, you should transfer or pay off any balance on your previous card, and close your previous credit card account.

If you have already paid €30 stamp duty in the current tax year – April 2 to April 1, your old credit card provider will issue a letter of closure to you when your account is closed.

This confirms that you have paid the stamp duty. The Financial Regulator advises that you send this letter to your new provider to make sure that you are not charged stamp duty again within the same year.

Remember, if you don't close your old account, then you will be charged €30 stamp duty on both accounts.

Finally, let me leave you with some good credit card housekeeping tips:

- Set up a direct debit from your account to pay the full amount due each month
- Don't get a card because it looks nice
- Keep your pin safe at all times
- Keep a record of your monthly statements
- Find out what interest rate you are being charged and try get a lower one
- Don't use the card for expensive purchases – term loans are cheaper
- If you have a mortgage, don't prioritise your credit card payment over your mortgage repayment

Liam's Action List

- The three words that will damage your finances to a point that is beyond repair are *minimum monthly repayments*. If you owe €8,000 and you want to spend the next fifty-four years paying it off, then pay the minimum amount each month.

- Credit card companies know that you usually do not pay more than they ask you for. They know that people do not understand how the compounding interest rate they charge you, along with the minimum payments due, really work. They thrive on your lack of financial education and knowledge and make billions each year in the process. So, resolve to pay them more than they ask for each month.

- You set your own limit. If you think the limit that you have is more than you are comfortable with, call up your provider and ask them to reduce the limit down to the amount you want it.

- How you stop using your credit card is a bit like giving up smoking. Hiding it in a safe place won't stop you from using it. Take out your credit card and just cut it in half.

- Try to negotiate with your present credit card company and ask them for a lower interest rate. If you have a good standing with them, they may agree to it. Ask them for the introductory rate rather than the standard rate. If they say no, then look at moving your card to someone else. You could go from 22.7 percent to 0 percent in less than a week.

- If you are in arrears on your credit card, ask your provider to freeze all charges and interest on your account immediately. They won't get all of the money they loaned you if they are adding fees and charges to an amount you are already having difficulty paying. They will sometimes agree to such requests.

- If you have cash on deposit and you can afford to clear your balance and still have money left over, then do it. Why pay 22 percent on your balance when you have money sitting in an account earning 1percent?

- If your chances of ever repaying a debt are slim, consider making an offer for full and final settlement of the amount you owe. If you owe €5,000 and you can't make the minimum repayment and haven't paid them a consistent amount over the last twelve months, and you have access to say €500, offer this to them. They may feel that based on your present circumstances, it is better for them to get this lump sum now rather than getting €5 per month from you for who knows how long. So don't be embarrassed to offer them an amount if you have it, you might be surprised by their reaction. But watch out – this will impact your credit rating.

'I've got all the money I'll ever need
if I die by four o'clock this
afternoon.'

–Henry Youngman

12

Shock and Awe – How to Destroy YourDebts

It is fair to say that a lot of people out there have no idea how much their loans are costing them in interest each month. Similarly, many people have no idea how to get out of debt, and automatically assume they have to keep their loan for the length of the terms dictated by their bank or credit union. This is simply not the case. That's what they would like you to think, whether you have a mortgage, car or personal loan.

People are not told by their banks how to structure what I call a debt elimination plan, but I am going to give you the tools and advice to get you started with your debt freedom plan. These two things will only get you half way through; the other 50 percent has to come from you. It is crucial that you stay focused and stay on track in order to accomplish this goal.

The aim is for you to clear your debts quicker than the terms of your loan allow and paying less interest to the bank in the process. This is achieved by what is known as the debt snowball and debt avalanche payment system.

Let me start with explaining what the debt snowball system. I will then show this in action and demonstrate what impact it can have on your finances.

The *Debt Snowball* system was first made popular by financial guru Dave Ramsey. What is advocated here is that people focus on paying off their debts one at a time, in order of the smallest balance first, with higher amounts of money being applied to each account in turn.

The idea is that you pay off the smallest debt first so that it will be paid off quickly, which psychologically generates momentum because you can see quick wins, and helps you to stay motivated and disciplined in paying off your remaining debts.

So, you pay off the smallest loan first and then after that is paid off, what you had been paying on that loan is used to increase the amount on your next loan and then when that is cleared off, you use that previous repayment amount towards your next debt and so on.

List all of your debts, in order of the smallest balance owed first. Pay the minimum amount you have to on all of your other loans except the first one on the list, because this is the one that you should pay as much towards as you can until it is paid off in full.

Once this loan is paid off, use that money to pay towards loan number two etc., and by doing this the amount you use towards your debts grows like a snowball (hence the name) rolling down a hill and your debts are paid off more quickly.

The *Debt Avalanche* works in exactly the same way as the snowball method, but this time it involves paying your debts off in order of the highest interest rate first. This is my favoured way of tacking debts.

Mathematically speaking, you will end up paying less interest in the long run when you concentrate on paying off loans first before smaller debts, unless most of your loans are at the same interest rate.

Let me show you the debt avalanche in action with real figures for clients I was working with recently.

They had the following debts in place:

Institution	Amount Outstanding	Monthly Repayment	Interest Rate
Credit Union 1	€ 3,587.28	€500	5.5 percent
Credit Union 2	€ 6,277.34	€600	4.95 percent
Credit Union 3	€ 6,566.86	€165	8.25 percent
Bank A	€ 5,400	€490.50	7.80 percent
Total	€21,831.48	€1,755.50	

If you look at the way their debt was structured, for Credit Union Loan 2, where there was €6,277 outstanding, they were paying €600 per month and the rate applicable was 4.95 percent, but Credit Union Loan 3 with a similar balance outstanding of €6,566 they were paying just €165 per month at a rate of 8.25 percent. It simply did not make sense to pay a lower monthly repayment on a loan that is charged at a higher rate!

The way their loans should have been structured was as follows:

Institution	Amount Outstanding	Current Monthly Repayment	New Monthly Repayment	Interest Rate
Credit Union 3	€6,566	€165	€600	8.25 percent
Bank A	€5,400	€490.50	€740.50	7.50 percent
Credit Union 1	€3,587	€500	€250	5.50 percent
Credit Union 2	€6,277	€600	€165	4.95 percent

You can see that I reversed the amounts on the first credit union loan and the last credit union loan. I reduced the repayments on their other credit union loan by €250 and applied them to the bank car loan. By doing this they accelerate the repayment of each loan.

After they clear the first credit union loan, they will then apply that surplus €600 to the bank car loan repayment and, once that is cleared, they apply that repayment amount to the next loan and so on.

It will look something like this for their first two loans:

Institution	Amount Outstanding	Monthly Repayment	New Monthly Repayment	Interest Rate	Paid in Full
Credit Union 3	€6,566	€600	€0	8.25 percent	Yes
Bank A	€5,400	€740.50	€1,340.50	7.50 percent	

By implementing the above, I calculated that they will clear Credit Union 3, which has a balance of €6,566, in eleven months as opposed to three years three months and this will save them a considerable amount in interest payments in the process.

Overall, by not spending any more money each month, their total debts were cleared two years earlier, saving them €1,478.51 in interest repayments in the process!

How to repay your loans faster, and with less money each year
Let me show you another example of how the snowball method works in real life, this time with a client of mine who was finding it difficult to repay his loans each year because he didn't have the income to do it. I restructured his loans using the snowball approach, which ended up him repaying his loans one year earlier and paying €7,000 less each year.

Let me show you what his position was:

Account Number	Balance Outstanding	Repayment	Expiry Date
123	€20,673	€7,500 per annum	2015
456	€20,098	€11,000 per annum	2014
789	€88,468	€13,200 per annum	2019
101112	€17,548	€4,800 per annum	2016
Total	**€146,787**	**€36,500**	

He had about €27,500 in farm grants mandated to the bank to repay his loans, but there was a shortfall of just under €9,000 each year that he simply could not afford to supplement. They completed a financial statement for their lender which confirmed this and showed that they were actually running quite a deficit each month.

I spoke with their bank and advised them that I believed their loans should be restructured as follows:

Account Number	Balance Outstanding	Repayment	Expiry Date	Paid on Schedule?
456	€20,098	€11,000 per annum	2014	Yes
123	€20,673	€7,500 per annum	2015	Yes
101112	€17,548	€4,800 per annum	2016	Yes
789	€88,468	€4,262 per annum	2016	Yes
Total	**€146,787**	**€27,562**		

By structuring their loans as I suggested, they will have the total amount repaid to their bank in six years one month, which is one year ahead of what the bank had planned for them. As each loan is cleared they transfer that repayment to the next loan and when that loan is repaid, they transfer that repayment to the next and so on. This will ensure that all of the loans are repaid ahead of schedule and with less money each year!

This is certainly not rocket science, but it took the lender a while to see that by simply restructuring the loans, they would get their money back in full. Albeit not as much in interest as they would have liked, but more importantly the loans were not going to get into arrears, which is where they were headed until I intervened.

Choose the right method for you

Remember that the snowball method starts attacking your debts with the *lowest balance first*. This is probably the best route if you want to see quick wins and, as I just showed you in my last example, you will see results very quickly.

The avalanche method starts with the *highest interest rate first* and is my favoured method of repayment, as it is designed to save you thousands in interest payments.

Look at your own situation and decide which option suits you best, but remember: the one option that is not open to you is to do nothing. Look at the difference that can be made to your debts using either method rather than just plodding along the way you are currently doing.

If you want to become debt-free as fast as possible, you have got to implement what I call the shock and awe system of repayments, which is snowballing or avalanching, and it starts by listing all of your debts on a blank sheet with the amount you owe, the interest rate charged, the minimum amount acceptable and the expiry date. When you do this it will probably become obvious, as we have seen in the examples above, that the way the loans are structured favours your lender rather than you. It is important to turn this situation on its head so that you are benefiting, and in many cases this is achieved by simply restructuring the way you pay your loans each month. If you can afford even a tiny overpayment each month on top of this, you are going a long and fast way to becoming debt-free.

Analyse your debts

Now we have come to probably the most fundamental area of the book: looking closely at your debts. One of the best ways to destroy any enemy is to study its nature, where it came from, how it survives and what it thrives on. So, we need to see your debt for what it really is, which means listing what it was for, the amount you owe, the interest rate, your monthly repayment and so on.

People often make hasty and rash decisions when they try to solve their debt problems. As a result they often end up paying off the wrong debts, in the wrong order, and at the expense of more important financial matters. The best approach is to first assess your overall financial position.

So, what I want you to do now is capture all of your debts on a worksheet. It should look something like this:

Debt	Balance Owed	Monthly Repay-ment	Interest Rate Charged	Purpose	Fixed or Variable	No. of Months taken to clear
Personal Loan	€3,671	€132.78	13.8 percent	Holidays	Variable	27
Credit Union	€3,850	€110.00	12.9 percent	Wedding	Variable	35
Car Loan	€12,567	€274.73	12 percent	2nd Card	Fixed	61
Home Improve-ments	€30,850	€450.00	7.3 percent	Double glazing and new kitchen	Variable	69
Credit Card	€4,500	€225	18 percent	God only knows!	Variable	47
Mortgage	€250,000	€1,320	4 percent	Home	Fixed	300

When I ask clients to complete this exercise, the initial reaction people have is fear; they feel like no one has as much debt as they do. However, after the wave of panic and nausea passes people become very determined to get to grips with their debt and all they need to begin is a plan of action.

When you look at your loans, some of them will strike you as being OK, i.e. your mortgage and maybe your home improvement loan, but others, like your sizeable car loan or your wedding costs, may make you stop and wonder why you ever borrowed so much.

It dawns on people that yes, they have made mistakes in the past, but they become resolved not to make them again in the future because the price they are paying now for those impulsive and casual decisions is just madness.

Remember in the future that there are two types of debt: good debt and bad debt. Good debt is borrowing money to purchase something that goes up in value, bad debt is everything else.

Back to the present and to reality. Now that you have listed your debt, you can start to see how they stack up. Here are some questions that will help you with this:

Are your loan rates competitive?
Compare these rates against what other lenders are offering. If you are paying above-average rates, you should think about moving to another lender if you can, or paying that debt off early.

Are you getting a tax break on any of your debts?
That home improvement loan, for example, may qualify for interest relief if the funds were borrowed to improve, repair or carry out refurbishments to your family home.

Are you vulnerable to interest rate increases?
Are the majority of your loans based upon a variable rate of interest? If rates were to increase, what impact would this have on your ability to repay? You should look at what fixed rates are on offer if you are worried about higher interest rates or lower income in the future.

Are your debts secured or unsecured?
A secure debt is one that the bank has some security against, i.e. a house or a car. The more security the bank has the better for you as the interest rate charged should be lower. That is one of the reasons credit card companies charge such a high interest rate.

Is there a specific date when you will be debt-free?
The reason I am suggesting this is because it is very important that you match up what debt needs to be repaid and when, because you may have to use funds towards another area of your financial life – for example, your sixteen-year-old child will be going to college in two or three

years' time, so it is important that your car loan is repaid before this happens in case you need to borrow money for third-level education or use your day-to-day income to fund the cost.

After you have answered these questions, you now need to decide which loans you need to get rid of first and this may be based on:

- Paying down the debt with the highest interest rate first

- Paying down the debt with the lowest balance first

- Paying down the debt with the fewest payments left first

- Paying down the debt you would most like to get rid of first

Your next step is to decide which debt is going to be your No.1 Target. It may look something like this:

Target	Loan
My No. 1 Target	Credit Card Loan
My No. 2 Target	Personal Loan
My No. 3 Target	Credit Union Loan
My No. 4 Target	Car Loan
My No. 5 Target	Home Improvement Loan

You now have to decide how much more you can commit, in addition to your minimum monthly payments, to your No.1 Target. Be practical here and decide realistically on the amount you can commit to each month.

So, now that you know what your debts are and what you are up against, let's look at what options are open to you to get rid of them as fast as possible. Having options is very important because what's best for one person may not be the ideal solution for everyone and, of course, this is the way it should be.

The important thing to consider before deciding on what route is best for you, is what are the advantages and disadvantages of each so that you know the whole truth before you act.

Let's now look at them one by one and review what each could offer you.

Liam's Action List

- List all of your debts in descending order of interest. This is your first step to getting rid of your loans as fast as possible. You need to know what you are up against, so list every loan, the amount owed, the interest rate, the date it will be paid off, etc.

- Resolve to spend less than you make. Easier said than done, I know, but you must stop using your credit cards and getting into more debt. Plan your spending before the month even begins, save up for large purchases and remember if you can't afford to pay for it today, you can't afford it full stop.

- Don't get carried away. Yes, be aggressive paying down debt as fast as you can, but don't get so ambitious that you neglect paying other bills such as your mortgage, rent, utility bills and so on.

- Any bonus payment or unexpected windfall, whether you know it was coming or not, use 50 percent of it to pay off your debt. Don't be tempted to spend all of it, or buy something useless with it, commit 50 percent of it towards your debts. The day after you receive it, pay off one of your loans, preferably the one with the highest rate. Don't think twice about it, just do it. Do as you please with the other 50 perent.

- After you have paid off one loan, don't just do nothing with the amount you used to be paying each month – use it as an overpayment on your next loan. This is the essence of the debt snowball principal and this is how you will pay off your loans in a much quicker way. You were used to paying it anyway, so continue paying it just this time on top of that other loan you have and then watch the amount you owe fall dramatically.

- Squeeze as much out of your budget as you can. Do whatever it takes to find extra cash so you can use that money towards your debts. A bit of pain in the short term will improve your finances to no end and once this debt is gone, you will free up more cash that you can use for whatever you want.

- Establish an emergency fund. Along with paying down your debt as fast as possible, don't neglect putting money away into your emergency fund either. Having this in place will prevent you from having to borrow again should you ever need money at short notice.

- Don't forget to reward yourself. As you get rid of loan after loan, take a moment to celebrate and go out and treat yourself to a nice meal, a night away, some new clothes or whatever it is you want, just remember to pay in cash!

'Debt is like any other trap, easy enough to get into, but hard enough to get out of.'

—**Henry Wheeler Shaw**

13

Five options for Getting Out of Debt

1. Debt Consolidation

This used to be a popular choice with people in the past, when banks were actually lending money, whereby people would use the value of their property to increase their mortgage in order to clear small, short-term debt and have one repayment at a much lower interest rate.

Upside
- Lowers your interest rate in some cases, i.e. credit card and other unsecured debt. Let's say you are paying 18 percent on a €10,000 credit card debt, if you are paying €150 per month it will take you twenty-four years before it is repaid in full. If you could consolidate this loan at say 5 percent and continued to pay €150 each month then it would be paid off in less than eight years.

- Lowers the number of creditors and payments you have to make each month – you just have one.

- Lowers your monthly payment, which can improve your cash flow with income now equal to or greater than your outgoings. This was probably not the case beforehand.

Downside
- It can and does create a false sense of debt reduction because there is only one monthly payment instead of the many you had prior to consolidation.

- In most cases when you lower your repayments you increase the amount of time you are paying the debt, which again creates another false sense of success.

- You lose equity in your property.

- You could 're-offend' if your problem is not cured at source, i.e. overspending – I see this happen all the time.

- You are putting your home at risk if you fail to make your repayments – you are effectively making unsecured debt secured debt and the consequences can be terrible.

- It is proving very difficult to get funds to consolidate debt from banks at the moment unless you owe less than 50 percent of what your home is actually worth.

2. The Rollover, Avalanche or Snowball method

I have covered this method already, but let me tell you again the pros and cons of using this method to clear your debt.

Upside
- It focuses you on getting rid of one debt at a time.
- You don't need much more money other than your existing minimum payments to get started.
- You get a great sense of achievement and success by seeing that you are clearing your debts quicker.
- You can save yourself thousands in interest by clearing your debts faster.

Downside

- If you choose to attack your loans based on the balance outstanding rather than the highest interest rate first then you may end up paying more in interest. However, in most cases the overall difference can be minimal.

3. Chasing Lower Interest Rates

This means transferring your debts to providers who will charge a lower interest rate from what you are currently being charged.

Upside

- With a lower interest rate you are increasing the amount of money that is actually going towards paying off your balance each month. We have already examined the difference this can make, particularly with credit card payments.

Downside

- Filling out forms can be a pain for some people, particularly credit card applications.

- You need to be aware that if you are offered a lower interest rate, it may only be for a specific period of time, i.e. six months, so you need to remeber when the interest rate is set to re-adjust so that you know when to repeat the process.

- It requires a lot of effort and is only applicable for credit card debt, as you will not be able to constantly refinance other debt. However, no one solution has to be for all of your debt – this method may very well suit your credit card debt and another method for your other loans.

4. Debt Relief, Debt Management Agencies

This strategy involves you retaining a debt management company to speak with all of your creditors on your behalf. They take the pain out of having to deal with creditors yourself, and they manage the process for you by lowering your debt payments each month after negotiating with your creditors for a lower monthly payment on each loan you have. While some debt management companies have good and honourable intentions, there are others, whom I refer to as financial predators, who exploit your lack of financial knowledge. They may be able to reduce your outgoings, but in the process they take a monthly fee that could have been used to actually pay down your debt.

Upside
- They may be able to lower balances outstanding or the interest rate charged to your account by negotiation with your creditor.

- You might even been able to give them a single payment each month and they then manage and distribute this between your various creditors. Unfortunately however, this can go wrong as well!

- They can get creditors to stop calling you at home and work and for many, that is reason enough to use this method.

- Creditors like working with financial professionals who may have a background in banking themselves. It is easier and quicker to find common ground when you are dealing with someone who understands the process better than you.

Downside

- Some debt management companies are nothing other than scams.They lack transparency and are unregulated, meaning they can collect high or hidden fees and charges from you and there is nothing you can do about it.

- Many times the plan created by the debt management company is created with their interest first and yours second, i.e. the more you pay each month, the more they get paid.

- These companies come and go; you might start off with a company that will not exist in six months and this lack of service and continuity can be a big problem.

5. Run and Hide

This is when you run away from your debts, hoping they will disappear without being repaid. Some people actually accomplish this by moving to another country until their creditor writes off the debt as a loss and gives up trying to collect it. Many people choose this option because they are moving away anyway because they can't find work at home. If they are planning on leaving anyway then why on earth should they be concerned about their debts? Read on . . .

Upside

- You won't have to pay your loans anymore.

- You won't be getting any more calls from your creditors unless you keep the same mobile phone.

Downside

- Your credit rating is destroyed and it will be a very long time, if ever, before you can secure finance again.

- Your creditors, if they are determined enough and the debt is large enough, may track you down.

- This strategy does not magically wipe out your debts in full, they will still exist.

- You will ruin the credit rating of a parent, brother or sister as well if you emigrate and refuse to repay the loan if they acted as guarantor for you in the first place. Not only will it impact their credit rating, they will end up having to pay the debt for you.

6. Use Savings to Clear Debt

This is a question that I am frequently asked, i.e. If I have a loan that I can afford to repay in full, should I do this and then save the monthly cost of my loan?

The best way to explain the answer is to use a real life example:

Amount you owe	€1,000
Rate you pay on debt	18 percent
Interest payment	€180
Amount on deposit	€1,000
Rate you earn on savings	3 percent
Interest received	€30

Upside

- If you pay off your debt, you will avoid paying interest of €180 over twelve months.

Downside

- If you put this same amount of money on deposit, it is effectively costing you €150.

- If you pay off your debt early and you are on a fixed-rate loan, you could be faced with an interest penalty.

- You could end up paying less in interest than what you could have made on deposit if the interest rate on your loan is lower than the amount you would get on deposit. For example, a client of mine had a tracker mortgage with around €60,000 outstanding and about nine years left to run – the amount of interest he would have to pay on this loan was approximately €2,500. But if he deposited this €60,000 it would have returned him over €12,000 in interest which was nearly five times more than what his loan was costing him.

- You could use up all of your savings to get rid of a loan and then when an emergency happens you have no funds to fall back on.

7. Bankruptcy and Personal Insolvency

In 2012, the Government introduced the much awaited and long overdue Personal Insolvency Bill. The act provides for a number of options that will be available when the bill is written into law.

The purpose of this bill is to provide for a humane way of dealing with the debt problems people are experiencing and, rather than dragging them through the court system, it provides for a non-judicial option, which is simply coming to an agreement with your creditors outside of the courts.

This non-judicial option has three elements:

1. One year debt relief notice

This allows for the writing off of unsecured debt, i.e. credit cards, personal loans etc, up to a maximum amount of €20,000. It is important to note that mortgage debt is not included in this area. In order to qualify for this relief, you have to meet a number of conditions first such as:

- Your net disposable monthly income is less than €60
- Your net assets are less than €400 (You can have a car which is not taken into account here provided it is worth less than €1,400)

If you meet the above criteria, your debt will be frozen for twelve months and then written off, provided your situation doesn't improve in the meantime.

You can only apply for two debt relief certificates in your lifetime.

2. Debt settlement arrangement

This part of the bill covers unsecured debts over €20,000 where some part of your debt could be written off over a five-year period. If this applies to you then you will need the assistance of a personal insolvency trustee. What happens in this case is that an application is made for a protection certificate that prevents your creditors from taking action against you for the next thirty days.

A proposal for the repayment of your debt is then made to your creditors. sixty-five percent of them must agree to the proposed payment plan and if they do, the arrangement will be recorded in an insolvency register.

If you stick to your repayment plan, then after five years the balance you owe to each creditor is written off.

You are only allowed one debt settlement arrangement in a ten-year period.

3. Personal insolvency arrangements

This proposal is to cover secured debts such as mortgages, as well as other unsecured debts and could be of great help to those people who are in serious mortgage difficulty. This arrangement is for people with debts of between €20,000 and €3 million.

Again a personal insolvency trustee is used to assist people in agreeing and overseeing a repayment plan that has to last for a period of six years although this may be extended to seven.

In order to qualify for this option, you have to demonstrate that you are currently insolvent and you are likely to remain so for the next five years. You make an application for what's called a protection certificate from the insolvency service, which prevents creditors from pursuing you for the next sixty days.

As before, you will have to get approval from your creditors and because you may have a mix of unsecured and secured creditors, the approval from each will be different, i.e. you need 55 percent agreement from your unsecured creditors and 75 percent from your secured creditors with the repayment plan you put forward.

The advantage to you in this case is that your mortgage lender, for example, is much more likely to agree to an honest repayment plan put forward by you than not, because the alternative could be bankruptcy, which will now only last for three years rather than twelve, as was the case before. The other big advantage here is that if you are in negative equity, then part of what you owe your lender could be written off under this arrangement. For example if you owe €300,000 and your house is worth €100,000, but you have the ability to repay a €200,000 mortgage, then the insolvency trustee may propose a debt reduction of €100,000.

If you have investment properties, they could be put up for sale and if you still owe more than what they were sold for, then a percentage of what is still owed will be repaid over six years and then discharged.

You can only apply for a personal insolvency arrangement once during your lifetime.

Bankruptcy

If you decide to declare yourself bankrupt, then you make a petition for bankruptcy to the court which will result in all of your property and assets coming under the control of an official assignee appointed by the court. What will then happen is that any income you earn in excess of a living expense you are allowed will be used by the courts assignee to pay off your creditors.

After a period of three years (at the court's discretion this could be extended by another five years) and provided you have been honest and co-operative at all times, you will then be discharged from bankruptcy.

I have no doubt that many people will, when the insolvency law comes into force, apply for arrangements that apply to their particular circumstances and it certainly will provide much needed relief for people who are genuinely struggling to make ends meet with debts they will never realistically be able to repay in their lifetime.

'If you think nobody cares if you're alive, try missing a couple of car payments.'

–Earl Wilson

14

Debt Prevention Safeguards

There are many rules or philosophies governing how we should use money. One such theory is known as the 'Law of 3', which suggests that if you want to achieve financial independence or improve your financial well-being, you need to focus on the following three things:

- Savings
- Protection
- Investments

Consider them each as a leg on a stool; if you only have two then the stool won't balance – you need all three to ensure financial independence. In this section, I am going to focus on the middle leg: protection.

When I discuss protection, I am generally referring to:

- Protecting your income in the event of illness
- Protecting your family in the event of your death
- Protecting your commitments in the event of serious illness
- Establishing an emergency fund

Even though you might be up to your eyes in debt and insurance is the last thing on your 'must have' list, you still need to consider all of your insurance options.

If you don't have insurance or enough of the right insurance, everything you own could be in jeopardy. A single sickness or accident could wipe you out. If you don't think it could happen to you, think again.

Of the sad facts of life is that things do not always go as planned. This is where insurance comes into play.

Insurance provides you with the financial assistance in the event that misfortune should strike. It is an incredibly important subject and is not to be taken lightly, so please listen up.

When I speak with people about this, the response is usually either: I don't need insurance or I can't afford insurance. I understand this but it is my belief that you can't afford *not* to have insurance. Another typical response is that people feel like they are being sold a product for the benefit of their broker, rather than for the benefit of themselves. Unfortunately, in many cases this is absolutely correct. The key though is understanding why you need to be covered and what type of policy is best suited to you. I will show you some examples of what you should consider in order to arrive at the right level of cover for you.

If you already have insurance cover that you do not need, then you are wasting money that could be used elsewhere. It would be more beneficial if this money was lodged in a savings account or used to pay down your debt, instead of into an insurance company's account.

However, if you do not have proper cover, you could be putting yourself, your family and your finances in grave danger. If you think getting out of debt is difficult when you are working and healthy, it is almost impossible if you are not adequately protected.

Life Assurance

You generally need life insurance only when others depend on your income, so if you fall into the following categories, you do not need life cover:

- Single people with no children
- Working couples that could maintain an acceptable lifestyle on one of their incomes
- Independently wealthy people who don't need to work
- Retired people who are living off their retirement income

If you fall into the above category, move on to the next chapter. If you don't, read on, it's very important.

Life assurance can be broken down into three major types:

- Mortgage Protection Cover
- Term Life Assurance
- Whole of Life Cover

Mortgage Protection Cover is a life policy that you are legally obliged to have when you take out a mortgage. It is assigned to your bank so that if you die, the amount outstanding on your mortgage is paid off in full – the cost reduces in line with your mortgage.

This is the cheapest form of cover you can get. However, I always come across people who have the wrong policy set up with their mortgage.

Example 1

I came across a client recently who gave me documentation surrounding his life assurance policy, as part of which he was paying €131.40 per month for mortgage protection.

The term remaining on his mortgage was approximately twelve years and he had about €40,000 outstanding on it. I showed him that if he was to arrange a policy for this amount based upon a decreasing form of cover, death benefit only, the monthly premium applicable to a new policy would be €13.75 per month. So, betweeen what he was originally paying (€131.20) and what he should have been paying (€13.75), there was a difference of €117.45 per month! That is a saving of €1,409.40 per year, or a saving of €16,912.80 over the term of the policy.

Just look at the options he now has available to him. He could use the amount saved to pay off his credit card debt; he could use it to reinstate his health insurance policy for him and his family; there are just so many things he could do to improve his finances, none of which would cost him anything more each month. He is just going to redirect what he was already spending his money on, but now in much better way.

This example is not unusual and not extreme. The majority of people I meet are paying way too much for cover and they assume there is nothing to be done about it.

Example 2

Another client of mine was paying €62.63 per month for a mortgage protection policy arranged via their bank.

When I compared the various providers in the marketplace, I found that the cost for covering their mortgage was €26.53 per month. So, the difference from what they were paying and what they could be paying was €36.10 per month. Not a life changing amount some might think, but it was a saving of €433.20 over the course of one year and €10,830 over the lifetime of the policy!

Let me put this small monthly saving into perspective. This amount each month would have the following impact for them:

- Accumulate a savings plan of €6,457 over a ten-year period
- Take fifteen months off the term of their mortgage as an overpayment, saving them over €6,765 in interest payments
- Add €50,951 to their retirement fund

So, when it comes to mortgage protection policies, keep them simple and pay as little each month as you need to.

Term Assurance – This is probably the best type of insurance you could take out because it is for a fixed term, at a fixed monthly premium.

It is the most appropriate because by the time the cover is over, i.e. at retirement age, your policy 'terminates' – the idea is that the mortgage should be paid, college will be done, and your kids will no longer be financially dependent on you.

You don't, therefore, need life assurance anymore because if you were to die, you would be able to support your spouse with your existing assets.

If that is not how you see life unfolding and you believe, because you have a special needs child or you want to use insurance to leave an inheritance and you want life assurance in place forever, then term assurance isn't for you.

If you fall into the other category, then it is best to arrange this type of cover.

Whole of Life Cover – This type of policy combines a death benefit with an investment component and is quite complicated and very expensive.

Here's the boring bit but it is important to know – the amount you pay each month goes into an investment fund, which is divided up into units, and the value of your policy and the life cover involved depends on how the price of these units move.

What happens with the life cover element is that the units are cashed in each month to pay for your life cover. At the start of this type of policy and the younger you are, assuming the investment return is good, the level of life cover can be maintained for the same premium probably for five or ten years.

However, after that the premiums are likely to go up and the premium is then reviewed every five years to make sure that the amount you pay each month is enough to maintain the level of life cover. If it isn't, your premiums will go up or your level of cover down!

How much cover do I need?

This will very much depend on your own particular circumstances. In this instance, one size does not fit all. Not everyone needs life assurance. If you are single and have no dependents then no one would be harmed financially by your death, so there is no real need to have life assurance, other than having your mortgage protected, if you have one.

If you are married and have children then the financial impact of your death could be significant, and life assurance is important. So, the questions are what type of policy is required and how much should you pay?

I cannot stress enough that there is no general guideline that suits everyone. When I carry out reviews for clients of mine and ask them how much cover they have and why they have that amount, the majority tell me that they have absolutely no idea, with the other small minority telling me that when they took out the policy in the first place, they were advised that it should be based on a multiple of their salary. What nonsense! The following factors have to be considered when arriving at an exact amount of cover that you specifically need:

-
- What is your net monthly income that needs to be replaced?
- What, if any, will your spouse receive from your pension?
- What is the widow's state pension?
- Is there any investment income your spouse would continue to receive in the event of your death? I.e. rental income, share dividends etc.
- How much do you currently spend on yourself each month?
- How much are your mortgage repayments?
- How much do you pay for insurance?
- What is your existing level of life cover?
- How old are your children?
- Will your spouse be entitled to a death in service benefit?
- How much have you got in savings?

All of these questions need to be answered first before you can arrive at a figure that is suitable to your particular circumstances. Only then will you know if you have either too much or too little cover.

Here are two examples of how to examine these factors in order to establish how much cover you need:

Example 1
If a fatal accident were to happen, your family would . . .
Need to cover your monthly income of c.€3,100

Less: monthly income payable on your death:
Employer's Pension c.€1,000
Widows State Pension (three dependent children) €1,226
Investment income (rental income, shares, dividends etc) €0

Less: monthly income no longer required:
Amount on self: €150
Mortgage repayments: €2,258
Insurance repayments: €220

Monthly Income Required/Shortfall: €1,754+
To compensate fully for this change would require a lump sum of €0 less:
Your existing level of life cover is €0 death in service benefit if any €105,000 liquid assets – cashed within 6 months €21,000

Additional life cover required: €0
In this example, there is no need for additional life cover because if the person were to die, their current income would have been replaced from various sources. So, if they took out a new life

policy they would be wasting money for cover they simply didn't need.

The next example, using the same method, showed that in this particular case, my client did in fact need cover.

Example 2
If a fatal accident were to happen, your family would . . .
Need to cover your monthly income of c.€2,900

Less: monthly income payable on your death:
Employers Pension c.€0
Widows State Pension (one dependent child) €968
Investment income (rental income, shares, dividends etc) €0

Less: monthly income no longer required:
Amount on self: €50
Mortgage repayments: €650
Insurance repayments: €60

Monthly Income Required/Shortfall: €1,172-
To compensate fully for this change would require a lump sum of €468,800 less:
Your existing level of life cover is €150,000
Death in service benefit if any €80,000
Liquid assets – cashed within 6 months €15,000
Which means additional life cover of €223,800

What we did then is arrange life cover in the amount of €220,000, which cost around €23 per month. The most important thing was that my client understood why they needed €220,000 worth of cover and had the comfort of knowing that the monthly premium of €23 was the absolute correct premium as they were neither over- nor under-insured; they were insured for the amount that was right for them.

Protection against serious illness

Next, I want to focus on protecting your income against your being diagnosed with a serious illness.

I received an email from a friend of mine recently who was diagnosed with cancer, not once but twice, and it was so powerful I just had to share it with you.

> *Hi, I am just back from my holidays and whilst there, I got to thinking – hard not to when lying out on the beach in glorious sunshine. Most of you now know that not alone did I have cancer in 2000 but again in 2010 so several operations later, lying on a beach for the first time since my operations, I was somewhat self-conscious to say the least. The decision I came to whilst lying out was this, why should I be hiding behind a beach towel? These scars are scars of survival. It is nothing to be ashamed of. Studies show that more and more people are surviving cancer and other serious illnesses. I was one of the lucky ones. Firstly for having survived cancer not once but twice and also to have had serious illness cover which allowed me to be in the fantastic position to have my mortgage paid off and to be able to afford holidays like that.*

If you consider the financial implications for you and your family in the event of you becoming seriously ill, it is very important to make sure you are protected against this eventuality, should it ever happen.

The statistics are frightening:

- Men have a 1 in 4 chance of becoming seriously ill before the age of sixty-five
- You are 3 times more likely to develop a serious illness before sixty-five than you are to die
- Women have a 1 in 5 chance of becoming seriously ill
- The most common illnesses are cancer, stroke and heart attack

The origins of the first Serious Illness Policy date back to 1983 in South Africa when the policy was launched on 6 October under the very threatening name of 'Dread Disease Insurance'. The name has undergone a number of changes over the years, from critical illness, to serious illness and even today some companies refer to it as 'specified illness'. Regardless of its name, the good news is that if you do suffer a serious illness, the chances of your surviving it are very good, but your lifestyle may need readjustment.

This type of policy will pay out a tax-free lump sum if you are diagnosed with an illness that is covered under your policy's specified illnesses. The most common illnesses covered by most companies and the most common illnesses that people claim under are: heart attack, cancer, coma, kidney failure, Alzheimer's, stroke, severe burns, loss of sight, surgery to aorta, kidney failure, major organ transplant, and multiple sclerosis.

Over the last number of years, the number of illnesses covered by a typical policy by life assurance companies has increased dramatically, with some companies now covering over forty different conditions.

Income protection

Finally, I want to show you how to insure your income. There is obviously never a right time to fall seriously ill or become involved in an accident. Most of us take our good health for granted and we do not expect a long-term illness or injury to happen to us, even if we all know someone it has happened to.

If someone is unable to work for whatever length of time, it can bring their earned income to a halt. 'It will never happen to me' is often the response I get when I suggest income protection to my clients, however, statistics tell a different story.

So, in the event of you not being able to work for a period of time, what would happen?

How long would your employer pay you? How much would they pay you? Do you know the answers to these questions? If you aren't sure of the facts, don't worry – you are not alone – the majority of people I speak with don't and those that think they know are almost always wrong.

Some employers calculate your pay as follows: 100 percent of your salary, minus social welfare payments, for the first twenty-six weeks of your absence; 50 percent for the next twenty-six weeks; and nothing thereafter, at which time you would have to rely on the state benefit of €188 per week.

This example is of an employer who has excellent cover in place for their employees. Please do not assume your employer is the same – they may not pay you a red cent if you are off work

– so find out what they would pay so that you can do something about it.

Of course there is a policy that can help you with this if you have no cover; it is called Permanent Health Insurance (PHI).

This is a protection offered by life assurance companies, that pays out should you suffer a loss of income by being unable to work due to a sickness or disability lasting longer than the deferred period under the policy.

The deferred period will typically be either thirteen, twenty-six or fifty-two weeks, so you must be out of work for at least the period chosen before the PHI income starts to be payable.

It is important to know that there must be a loss of income in order for a PHI benefit to become payable, it is not enough just to be sick.

You can claim tax relief on PHI premiums, up to an annual limit of 10 percent of your income. You can get immediate tax relief on PHI premiums from a deduction in your wages.

The benefit is taxable in the hands of the policyholder and is payable until the policyholder is fit to return to work up to a maximum age, usually sixty or sixty-five.

So, you could take out an income protection policy which would replace up to 75 percent of your current salary, less social welfare benefits.

Let me give you an example of how this works in real life:

Let's assume your salary is €50,000 per year and you can protect this up to 75 percent, i.e. €37,500 minus social welfare, so the amount you need to cover is €27,600.

I am going to show you what can be done to protect your income and what would happen if we didn't.

No Benefits in Place

	Annual Benefit	Monthly Benefit	Weekly Benefit
State Benefit	€9,776	€814.66	€188

Benefits in Place

	Annual Benefit	Monthly Benefit	Weekly Benefit
Income Policy	€27,600	€2,300	€531
State Benefit	€9,776	€814.66	€188
Total	€37,376	€3,114	€719

You can see the benefit of having this in place and what would happen if you didn't.

The cost of putting this in place was €23.02 net per month, or €0.76 per day.

You can see how exposed your income could be by not being able to work for a period of time and you can also see that it can be relatively inexpensive to put it in place. Of course the nature of your job will have an impact on your monthly premium and there are many occupations that cannot get this type of cover because they are perceived to to be high risk, i.e. the chances of making a claim are higher than others. I want you to find out do you need it and if you do how much it will cost you.

Having insurance cover in place is very important and it is one that many people fail to understand because they don't see an immediate value or a tangible benefit to it and consider it a waste of money. Believe me it is not. It is crucial that you have the right form of cover in place so that if anything was to happen, your financial life would not be severely impacted.

I have come across so many people who decided to become debt-free, implement their plan and everything is going well when BANG, an illness or injury prevents them from earning an income and they simply can't survive on what the state pays them. They go from being on track to clearing their debt, to increasing their debt in the blink of an eye because they have to borrow money all over again just to make ends meet.

Don't let this happen to you.

Establishing your emergency fund

Many people in Ireland today are living pay cheque to pay cheque and, before the month even begins, the money is gone. People tell me all the time that if they are paid weekly, it is lodged into their account on a Friday and gone again the following Tuesday. If this sounds familiar then you are not alone.

The consequence of this, however, is that many people have little or no savings, have no financial cushion so to speak, and the smallest financial disaster like needing new tyres for the car, for example, can leave you high and dry with nowhere to turn.

I have already referred to the importance of having an emergency fund in place, but it is necessary to stress just how important it is to have in place, so much so that I would consider it more important to establish your emergency fund before you even begin to tackle your debts.

You can call it what you like, an emergency fund or a rainy-day fund, but I like telling people that they should consider it their *financial first aid kit.*

The financial first aid kit is meant to be used when something unforeseen happens that must be treated or resolved quickly to prevent it becoming an even bigger problem, i.e. you accumulate more debt to pay for those tyres, or the NCT test, or whatever it is that you need this money for.

Start with a small amount, even if you can only put aside €5 each week or month, just Start. Getting into the habit of putting money away will give you a boost and you know what? Money attracts money, suddenly you will discover more money and by the time the year is finished you will have much more than you ever thought you would. If you have no money, not even a few euros, money will not come your way, it will just pass you by, it won't even come and say hello.

Liam's Action List

- Are you paying too much for life cover? If you answered 'I don't know' then you are almost certainly are. Do you even need it? Get out the policy you have that may be assigned to your mortgage and check to make sure that you are not paying more than you need to. The chances are high that you can reduce your outgoings so speak with an independent financial advisor and ask them to get quotes for you.

- Find out from your employer how much they would pay, if any, if you died whilst in their service. Normally, a multiple of about three or four times your salary would be paid to your next of kin if you died in service.

- Do you know how much of your salary your employer would pay you and for how long if you were unable to work due to an accident or illness? Could you survive on €188 each week if they didn't pay you anything? Don't wait until it's too late to find out.

- There is a one in three chance – repeat, a one in three chance – that someone will suffer a serious illness before they reach the age of sixty-five. You are more likely to suffer a serious illness than you are to die, so look at the cost of having some form of serious illness/disability protection in place. As a rule of thumb the amount of cover you should have is one or two times your annual salary.

- Make your will. If you die without making a will, the law will decide what happens to your estate, and in some cases what will happen to your children if you and your partner die together. Contact a solicitor and make an appointment with them to formally put your will in place.

'Ten million dollars after I'd become a star I was deeply in debt.'

—**Sammy Davis, Jr.**

15

Debt Strategies for Everyone

I hope that having read this far, you have been picking up lots of tips that you can apply to your particular needs, whether that is paying off your mortgage early, eliminating your credit card debt, saving money, creating a spending plan and so on.

I want to focus now on what particular strategy you should be adopting, based on your current age and situation.

There are a number of financial stages and although you personally might not pass through them all, some will certainly apply. They are:

- Freedom of Youth
- The Family Years
- Middle Age
- Anxious Middle Age

Each phase is characterised by a different set of opportunities and demands that will determine the financial decisions you make. What you should do is not set in stone, and what is right for one person may be quite wrong for another.

For example, re-mortgaging and extending the term of your mortgage does not make sense for someone who is nearing retirement. Equally, racking up credit card debt can become financial suicide at a very young age for someone just out of college.

For each phase in your life, your priorities and what you should be focusing on may look something like this:

Freedom of Youth:

This is the early phase of your life, when you stop having to rely on your parents and, all being well, you start to earn your own living. Typically, no one is dependent on you and your main priority is having a roof over your head. Quite possibly rented accommodation fits in with your desire for mobility.

My best advice to anyone at this stage is to learn about money. Hopefully reading this book will help to set you on the right road. If, however, you are not in your twenties but your son or daughter is, I would encourage you to give them this book and ask them to read it. It will stand them in great stead for their future.

When you think about it, at this stage of life a person may have spent the last five or six years studying, learning a different language, getting their degree or masters. They are incredibly knowledgeable about the area they studied in but what do they know about budgeting, goal setting, debt, saving for retirement? Nothing, and all those years of hard work may come to nothing because if they get into debt, it could take them years to get out of it, as we have seen. So this stage in your financial life is about prevention.

In your twenties, you really should not have many commitments other than maybe a student or car loan, so the net result should be a surplus of income over expenditure. The temptation of youth, we know, is probably to spend the excess, but there are some bones you can build into your skeleton even now. In a realistic order of priorities, these are:

- Emergency fund to draw on if you face unexpected expenses
- Protecting your income in the event of illness
- Pension planning – it takes a lot of investment to build up an adequate pension, so the earlier you start the better (see the section on the 60 Percent Solution on page 76
- Start saving for short-term saving – e.g. for a car, holidays etc.
- Start saving for medium- to long-term saving – e.g. eventual deposit for house purchase
- Get health insurance
- Pay your bills on time, all of the time

The Family Years

Most people, at some stage in their lives, will marry or live with a partner. This creates a different financial situation. Even if your partner is financially independent, you are likely to develop some joint commitments. They may be, for example, sharing the costs of buying or running a home, in which case you have to consider what the financial impact on your partner would be if you were to die.

For those with children, your shared commitments are even more demanding. There will be greater pressure on your resources at this stage than at any time of your life. If you or your partner stop working, are made redundant or cut back on your work in order to care for your children, these resources will further be depleted.

In this situation it is important to:

- Build an emergency fund
- Protect your own and your partner's income in the event of illness, at least to the extent that joint expenses would be covered
- Keep on top of your credit cards and any other consumer debt you might have
- Take out life insurance on your own and your partner's life
- Borrow money only for things that go up in value, not down
- Start planning for future educational costs, they may be eighteen years away, but if you start early enough you will not be under so much pressure later in life
- Plan your pension – ideally this should have a higher priority but this might not be possible if funds are tight
- Start a short-term savings plan for family events, such as presents, holidays, Christmas etc.
- Invest in long-term savings accounts – if you have any money left that is!

Middle Age

This is the time in your life when you should be looking to become mortgage- and debt-free. The financial demands of a family should subside, and you may enter a phase where you have more disposable income. This, therefore, would be a good time to look at future events, but if you choose to simply concentrate on the present, then you may increase your spending, go on more holidays etc.

At this stage your priorities might look like this:

- Emergency fund if not already in place
- Get serious about paying off your mortgage and other loans in full
- Protecting income against illness
- Fun targets – more holidays, hobbies, a second home and so on
- Pension planning

Anxious Middle Age

Unfortunately, the relaxed feeling of early middle age tends to give way as you enter your fifties. It begins to dawn on you that retirement is just around the corner, and perhaps you should be doing more to prepare for it. Pension planning should now move up your priorities and for the first time, your thoughts might turn to the threat of health problems associated with old age.

At this stage, you might also find elderly parents becoming more dependent on you, though equally, your resources might be boosted through inheritance.

The following priorities might be:

- Pension planning
- Long-term care planning, if you are not confident of adequate state provision
- Serious investment
- Protecting your nest egg

'I'm not a paranoid, deranged millionaire. Goddamn it, I'm a billionaire.'

–**Howard Hughes**

16

The Financial Habits of Wealthy People

For most of us, achieving long-term financial success, whatever it may mean to you, is like being on a journey. You see, few people get financially independent quickly and those that do often don't manage to maintain their new-found status because they simply weren't sufficiently prepared. This is not a negative statement, but rather my request to you to take charge of your finances and prepare well in advance, so that when the opportunities arise, you have the ability and confidence to take advantage of them.

In order to increase your chances of making this happen, I will now detail the characteristics and habits that most financially successful people use throughout their lives and, if you recognise what they are and apply them to your own situation, I guarantee you that they will have a profound impact on your financial success.

1. Successful people have powerful belief systems

Louise Hay is a world-renowned author who lectures in metaphysics. She once said that 'if we don't believe something is possible, we find all sorts of obstacles to get in our way'. She's right, isn't she? Because if we believe something to be true we ultimately decide if we want to make it happen or if we don't. Henry Ford also said, 'Whether you believe you can or you can't, you're right'. These are very powerful words from a man who changed the way we live simply by turning an idea into something tangible – a mass-produced car.

Henry Ford is also credited with saying 'If I asked my customer what he wanted, he would have said a faster horse'.

I can give you all the advice in the world when it comes to your finances, but if your belief doesn't support what you want to achieve, then all the advice and tools in the world will do you no good. For example, if I show you how to get out of debt, but you believe that debt isn't bad or that low monthly repayments allow you to afford things more easily, you will continue to find ways to get back into debt.

2. Financially successful people consistently spend less than they earn

There are two things you can do with your money: you can save it or spend it on the things you want and need. As is pointed out earlier in this book, sometimes we fool ourselves into thinking we need something we really just want it. Financially successful people know that the number one key to financial success is actually very simple – to consistently spend less than they earn and save the difference. The key standard they use is to save a minimum of 10 percent of their net monthly income.

I read a book recently called *The Richest Man in Babylon*,

throughout which the author, George Clason, sets the minimum standard for saving at 10 percent. This book, often referred to the as the bible of personal finance, tells us that following this principle will shift our psychology to that of a successful money manager and a person of wealth and comfort.

Spending less than you earn is also referred to as LBYM – Living Below Your Means – and can be applied regardless of your level of income.

People often use their income as an excuse for not applying this principle. I often hear 'if I had more money I would have a better plan' from clients and my reply is always the same; 'if you had a better plan you would have more money'.

Who's smarter with their money, a person earning €100,000 per year but spending €100,000 as well or the person earning €30,000 and spending €20,000 and saving the difference? If that person earning €100,000 was now earning €110,000 guess what their outgoings would become? Yes, you got it, €110,000.

It's not the amount you earn that will make you rich, it's the amount you save that will.

By the way, very few self-made millionaires drive new cars, they normally drive three- or four-year-old cars. They don't outwardly look very wealthy but they don't care about impressing you, they care about being financially secure and independent, and therefore recognise that spending less than they earn will help them achieve this. You should take a leaf out of their book.

3. Successful people use words that create success

This doesn't just apply to your finances, it can apply to any area in your life. Much like our beliefs, words can inspire us or they can tear us down. When it comes to our finances, the words we use to describe who we are, what we want to achieve, or what holds us back can have a huge impact on our financial affairs. I really believe that the words we use to describe our financial condition more often than not will *become* our financial condition. So, choose your words wisely. Over the years, I've heard a number of negative phrases used by people when asked how they are doing financially, such as: 'getting by', 'hanging in there', 'holding it together', 'robbing Peter to pay Paul', 'making ends meet' and so on.

I know this is tough to do, particularly when times might be difficult, but remember, you are what you say, so speak powerfully, positively, and with a vision of how you want things to be. Remember what I said at the start of this book – I am going to be debt-free. How do you feel when you say it? Positive, right? What if you say 'God I'll never clear that credit card off' or 'I need to win the lottery to sort myself out'? How does it make you feel? If you continue saying these things you will never improve your finances.

4. Financially independent people always ask questions that lead to success

Tony Robbins, the famous motivational author, said in his book *Awaken the Giant Within*, that 'if you want to have a better quality of life, ask a better question'.

What if you started asking yourself some of the following questions:

- Have I considered the cost of borrowing and how it will affect my overall financial plan?

- Do I need this item or is it something I want and can really do without?

- Would the money I'd be paying in interest be better off invested?

- Where is this money coming from? Have I earned it or do I still have to work for it?

- Have I considered how much I can save if I save the money first, then come back next year and buy it for cash?

Before purchasing something, wealthy people ask themselves these types of questions to help them focus on the total cost or the consequences of their actions.

5. Financially astute people look at problems in a different way

This is an old question but it's a good one, so tell me which problem would you rather have?

A Not being able to pay your €400 rent payment

B Not being able to pay your €4,000 mortgage payment

I hope you picked B, if you didn't you might want to consider a change in your philosophy regarding financial problems. One of my favourite authors Jim Rohn explained the principle behind this wealth characteristic very well when he said: 'Don't wish your problems were easier, wish you were better'.

Financially successful people don't run away from their financial problems either, they see them as a challenge that needs to be overcome and they find ways of overcoming them. Whereas others might run away from the problem because it seems too difficult, financially successful people find out what needs to be done and they do it. Take pension planning for instance. I always find people giving out about the value of their pension and how much it has dropped in value etc, but they do nothing about it. Financially successful people will do something about it; they will read up on the subject, they will seek advice, they will choose a strategy that works for them so that if anything was to happen again in the stock market, their fund would be protected whilst others who did nothing will continue to suffer.

6. Financially independent people treat their personal finances like a business

Let me ask you a question: if your personal finances were a business, would your friends and associates want to invest in you? Imagine you are self-employed and you have to pay the wages at the end of every month, would you pay someone who obviously didn't care about how well the business was performing or was not putting any effort into their job? Of course you wouldn't, but when you look at how you manage your own finances, are you that person who just doesn't care or pay any attention to your money each month?

Again, looking at it from a business perspective, do you have more money saved and invested at the end of the year than you had at the beginning? Is that not the goal of running a business – to make money at the end of your year? I want you to start treating your finances like a business and acting as if this business is building financial independence for yourself and your family.

7. Financially successful people understand the law of urgency and scarcity

One of the reasons people are in debt today is simply that they spent more than they earned and used credit to bridge the difference. The reason this happened to so many people was because they got suckered into buying products and services they didn't really need and organisations preyed on their vulnerability. These organisations understand how people's minds work and use scarcity and urgency as subconscious tools.

They use phrases like 'Hurry, before this offer ends'; 'Only two days left'; 'Don't miss out'; 'Sale ends Saturday'. I know of a shop, for example, that has a poster in its window that says 'Sale ends in 2 days', which has been there for two years. This phraseology is designed to entice us to part with our money so it is important to recognise these marketing strategies when you see them and not to get caught up in the false sense of urgency they are trying to convey.

Financially successful people are not fooled by the scarcity and urgency that banks and retailers promote. A good friend of mine who inherited some money recently went to his local bank and deposited it with them. The manager asked to see him and suggested he open a particular account with them. However, the manager warned that his money would need to be in this account by Friday, which was three days later, otherwise he would lose out on the opportunity. My friend sensed that this urgency from the bank manager was strange and felt a bit under pressure to open the account. Luckily he didn't, because the account in question was not suitable for him, the bank manager just wanted to create a false sense of urgency so that he would keep his money with the bank and not move it anywhere else. This is a sad state of affairs but unfortunately true.

So it is important remember this law of scarcity and urgency. As I said to my friend, if you did miss the deadline for that account, don't worry; another account will come along which will be practically identical to the one you didn't open. Two weeks after the closing date a new account was launched, identical to the previous one.

8. Financially successful people do not gamble or play the lottery

I come across so many people who are hoping that one day something miraculous will happen that will solve their financial problems. Some people think this is winning the lottery, inheriting money, getting a pay rise and so on. They don't do the simple, everyday small steps that are needed because they are waiting for the big bang. Saving for retirement is a prime example of this. Rather than saving small amounts each month, they are waiting to sell their business, or for the big return on their investment to help them. If you don't have a financial plan that you constantly work at, and you don't have that positive mindset, no amount of money will actually solve your problems.

9. Financially successful people don't let setbacks hold them back

Financially successful people who over time got themselves in a position where they are financially independent, also had their own setbacks, losses and failures along the way. However, they used these setbacks to their advantage and learned from them.

Yes, they had failures, but that didn't put them off striving to achieve their financial goals because nothing was going to stop them from becoming financially independent.

I was speaking with a self-made millionaire recently and I asked him what was the one thing that had gotten him where he was today and the answer at first surprised me. Rather than saying his new online business made him what he is or a particular investment did very well for him, he said that initial failures when setting up some businesses in his early twenties were his biggest asset and the single reason he was wealthy today. He said if you constantly focus on what you have learned in the past and see how it can benefit you in the future, then you can turn those setbacks into your advantages.

I am sure that there are many more characteristics I could list of those who have been financially successful. You might have noticed that I haven't referred to financially successful people as being wealthy because it is important not to judge your success or happiness by what the balance is in your bank account. I believe you judge your success by being able to do whatever it is that you want to in life, to follow your dreams and passions and being beholden to nobody or no organisation. If becoming debt-free makes that happen, then great. So I think knowing how people who have financial freedom think and act is very important so that you can learn from them and apply those lessons in your own finances, because you will improve your bottom line to no end.

The Last Word

The reason I wrote this book is simple: I believe that people need help making smart financial decisions. They don't want gimmicks, they don't want information they can't act upon, they don't want someone to talk down to them in a condescending or patronising way, they want simple honest advice that they can relate to and that if acted on, will improve their financial lives in a way they never ever imagined.

However, because this book is about money and personal finances, I was conscious not to give the impression that money is the only important thing in life or that it should be your only focus. It isn't and never should be, but money has a way of impacting on our lives and that is why it is so important that we take control of it, rather than let it control us.

So, this book is about getting your financial affairs in order and the lessons and examples it contains have all been experienced and learned by me and the many thousands of people I have coached in the past twenty years. If you work hard at your finances and do as I say, I am very confident that you will get your finances under control.

When I sat down to write this book, my first objective was to coach, motivate, inspire, share my knowledge and my real-life experiences, and provide much more than just information about how to improve your situation. Information alone will do nothing to improve your finances. The purpose of this book is to transform your financial life by providing you with the tools that, if acted upon, will make a difference to you and your family's quality of life. I know this works, not just because it worked for me, but because of the thousands of people I have worked with over the years that are now financially independent.

Reaching the end of this book will hopefully signal the beginning of a fantastic financial future for you. Yes it may be difficult at times, but stick with my advice; it works and I am confident that you can do it.

Your behaviour and attitude to money is the key to your success. It is not what you already know, learn and intend to do from reading this book; it is what you do now that will determine your outcome.

The amount of money you earn is not the key to financial success, the amount you keep is. Please remember that. Being sensible about money means you have the ability to look at the long-term consequences of actions and decisions you make right now. Stay focused on the big picture view of your life rather than living day to day, and delay short-term gratification for those long-term benefits you want to achieve.

When I speak to audiences about personal finance matters, I always tell them that if they want to improve their situation, they have to be willing to learn in order to gain knowledge. Yes, experience is a great teacher but only if you have been listening! A lot of people think they know everything there is to know about financial matters and aren't willing to learn anything new. Often, these same people are struggling financially. The Buddhists say that when you think you know everything, that's when you know nothing. When you think you know nothing, that's when you start to know something.

We hear so many terrible stories about how people are struggling financially in Ireland today. For some it is a comfort to know they are not alone, but this herd mentality will not give you financial security, it will give you nothing. Break away from the pack and do something about your life. Start now.

Use what you have learned in this book, share it with others if you feel they will benefit. I have no doubt that our paths may cross one day, and that when we meet, you will share with me your success stories. Until then, I wish you the very best in your journey toward financial freedom.